European and Transatlantic Studies

Springer
Berlin
Heidelberg
New York
Barcelona
Budapest
Hong Kong
London
Milan
Paris
Santa Clara
Singapore
Tokyo

Titles in the Series

B. Eichengreen, J. Frieden, J. v. Hagen (Eds.)
Monetary and Fiscal Policy in an Integrated Europe

B. Eichengreen, J. Frieden, J. v. Hagen (Eds.)
Politics and Institutions in an Integrated Europe

João Loureiro

Monetary Policy in the European Monetary System

A Critical Appraisal

Acting Editor: Jürgen von Hagen

With 57 Figures
and 13 Tables

Springer

João Loureiro
Assistant Professor
University of Porto
Faculty of Economics
Rua Dr. Roberto Frias
P-4200 Porto, Portugal

ISBN 3-540-60784-6 Springer-Verlag Berlin Heidelberg New York

Die Deutsche Bibliothek – CIP Einheitsaufnahme
Loureiro, João:
Monetary policy in European monetary system/João Loureiro. – Berlin; Heidelberg; New York; Barcelona; Budapest; Hong Kong; London; Milan; Paris; Tokyo: Springer, 1996
(European and transatlantic studies)
ISBN 3-540-60784-6

Printed in Germany

SPIN 10518801 43/2202 - 5 4 3 2 1 0 – Printed on acid-free paper

Acknowledgments

Most of the literature recently produced on European monetary cooperation focuses on the challenges of transforming the European Monetary System (EMS) into a European Monetary Union. However, a number of issues related to the EMS itself are yet to be clarified. Hence my decision to look backwards. This book is the result. It addresses questions that, so far, have only been explored superficially, if at all.

The final product benefited, at different stages, from comments by Clas Wihlborg, Boo Sjöö, Dick Durevall and Paul De Grauwe. Richard Sweeney and Alek Markowski also provided me with helpful comments on different chapters. To all of them I owe thanks. The same applies to seminar and conference participants at Gothenburg University, Gilleleje, Thessaloniki University and St. Andrews University where preliminary versions of some of the chapters were presented. I am also grateful to Jürgen von Hagen and Michael Fratianni both for inviting me to publish in this series and, as editors, for the useful comments and suggestions for revisions and extensions. Remaining errors and omissions are, of course, my sole responsibility.

Finally, I would like to acknowledge the hospitality and financial support of Gothenburg University where most of this work was produced. Financial support and the appropriate environment to complete this book was also provided by the Faculty of Economics at the University of Oporto with which I am currently affiliated.

Oporto, January 1995.

João Loureiro

Editor's Introduction

The European Monetary System was started in 1979 to create a *zone of monetary stability* in Europe and to prepare the way for Europe's monetary unification, an old dream of the protagonists of European integration. After an initial phase of difficulties marked by frequent realignments, the EMS had its high tide in the second half of the 1980s, when even sceptics admitted that the EMS apparently helped former high-inflation countries in Europe to regain monetary stability.

The proposition that – in contrast to the original intentions which emphasized the symmetry of the new system in which monetary decisions were to be made by collective agreement – the EMS allowed the German Bundesbank to dictate the terms of monetary policy to Europe was an essential element of this view. In the early 1990s, the EMS suddenly collapsed under the pressure of speculative attacks on the weaker currencies. Although it formally continues to operate, the exchange rate constraints are no longer effectively binding, leaving the EMS as a vehicle for unilateral commitment to a pegged DM exchange rate. In the coming years, the member countries of the European will have to decide whether or not they want to return to a binding exchange rate system on their way to a monetary union.

A careful analysis of how the EMS worked is an essential requirement to answer that question. The benign view of the EMS as an instrument for countries with a history of high inflation rates to gain credibility of their new commitment to price stability and reduce inflation rates without suffering high unemployment has so much dominated the policy debates in the early 199s, that policymakers, like many economists, had no other explanation of the breakdown of the system than the vicious activities of a small club of cynical speculators. In that view, Europe should return quickly to the tight exchange rate constraint and protect it by limiting internatinal capital mobility.

This is where Joao Loureiro's study comes in. Loureiro provides us with a rigorous and refreshing empirical assessment of the EMS. He focuses his attention of three critical questions: how did the EMS member states resolve the conflict between exchange rate management and the control of domestic monetary conditions, to what extent did the Bundesbank dominate European monetary policy, and how much credibility did the high-inflation countries gain by being members of the EMS?

Loureiro's answer to the first question is based on an analysis of the sterilization of foreign exchange interventions in the EMS. By showing that most EMS central banks sterilized significants parts of their interventions, he demonstrates that these policymakers were never willing to subordinate their domestic policy goals under the requirements of a fixed exchange rate policy. In other words, the system was inherently unstable because it had to exist with an unresolved internal conflict. Viewed from this perspective, the speculative attacks only uncovered the fundamental inconsistency of the system and this inconsistency ought to be solved if the next attempt at fixed exchange rates in Europe is to be more successful.

Loureiro's answer to the second question is equally contradicting the benign view of the EMS. Using a variance-decomposition of the domestic component of the monetary base in each EMS country, he shows that most countries retained their monetary autonomy even in the EMS. This paves the way to an answer to the third question. Here, Loureiro shows on the basis of estimated Phillips-curve trade-offs that the credibility gains facilitated by the EMS were at best moderate.

The insights provided by this study carry an important message for international monetary policy. They tell us that the hope to cure weaknesses of national monetary policy by relying solely on the external constraints of a fixed exchange-rate system remains an illusion. Of course, this does not imply that there is no role for exchange-rate pegging as a monetary strategy. However, a successful solution to the problems of monetary instability and lack of credibility must begin at home and involve a reform of domestic monetary institutions.

Jürgen von Hagen

Contents

CHAPTER 1
Introduction

There is some dispute in the literature on whether exchange rate instability is or is not a negative factor for the development of international trade and, through it, economic growth. Despite the existence of international financial instruments for hedging, exchange rate uncertainty is sometimes considered to cause frictions in free trade.[1] The fear that exchange rate volatility might disrupt European trade and work against the European Economic Community (EEC) has haunted proponents of European integration since the 1950s.

A particular reason requiring exchange rate stability among EEC countries relates to the *common agricultural policy* (CAP). Under the rules of the CAP, the prices of the European agricultural goods are fixed in terms of a common currency, the *European Unit of Account* later labeled *European Currency Unit*. These prices are then translated into domestic currency prices according to the prevailing exchange rates. Exchange rate fluctuation would, thus, be destabilizing for production and trade of agricultural goods.

The issue of creating sheltered foreign exchange markets for European currencies became more pressing at the end of the 1960s. Waking events were the major exchange rate realignments within the Bretton Woods system carried out by France and Germany. Given that agricultural goods had a common currency fixed price, the avoidance of distortions in trade was smoothed through a scheme of *"monetary compensatory amounts"*. This scheme, however, gives rise to undesirable implications for the EEC budget.

Another, related reason for the creation of an exchange rate system for Europe had to do with the fears that EEC countries could respond in different ways to the high inflation run by the United States. Non-convergent attitudes by member countries could endanger the process of full economic integration as proposed by the Werner Plan of 1970. This plan proposed the creation of an Economic and Monetary Union with full currency convertibility and irrevocably fixed exchange rates to be achieved by the end of the 1970s. As a transitory step, the margins of fluctuation of intra-EEC exchange rates should be reduced. This was done first with the "Snake in the Tunnel", that was later developed into the "Snake". Since March 1979, monetary cooperation has been carried out under the European

[1] The mixed evidence on the effects of exchange rate volatility on trade flows can be exemplified with a study by the IMF (1984) and a study by Cushman (1986). While the latter finds volatility effects on trade, the former does not find any negative correlation between the two variables. For a general discussion on exchange rate variability and its implications for trade, see De Grauwe (1989), chapter 12.

Monetary System (EMS). At present, there are plans to transform the EMS into a European Monetary Union (EMU), the last stage in the process of complete monetary integration.

The reasons given above to justify the European exchange rate arrangements can be taken as political. Trade integration was just a first step into complete European integration and was not to be jeopardized by exchange rate instability. It is, thus, the idea of a Single Europe, a unified block, that lies behind European exchange rate schemes. One indication for this strong political component can be taken from German membership in the EMS. The Bundesbank strongly opposed the formation of the system. The German authority deciding on participation in international exchange rate arrangements, however, is the Ministry of Finance. Thus, the EMS was politically imposed on the German central bank.

Besides political reasons, other explanations have been offered to justify participation in the EMS. One is that the system is a framework for economic cooperation which prevents the individual use of exchange rate policies to achieve national output and inflation goals. This explanation is, however, in conflict with another view of the EMS, the view that the EMS imposes discipline on the high-inflation participants. According to this hypothesis, high-inflation countries join the EMS to adjust inflation to the leading low-inflation member, Germany; an adjustment that lowers the cost of disinflation compared to similar policies carried out outside the EMS.

The analysis of European monetary cooperation in recent years has focused on the gains, costs, and the appropriate steps towards EMU. However, there are questions related to the working of the EMS that are yet to be clarified. This book consists of a set of empirical analyses of the operation of the EMS before the Summer of 1992, when the system collapsed. The book focuses on issues that have not been explored so far and also delves deeper into some other issues that have only been analyzed in a superficial way. The organization is in eight chapters, of which chapters 3-7 contain the empirical studies. These chapters are preceded by a brief summary of the origins, design and factual working of the EMS in chapter 2 and are closed with a summary and conclusions in chapter 8.

Chapter 3 analyzes exchange market interventions by EMS central banks during the first decade of the system. According to the design of the EMS, official interventions in the foreign exchange market are the only explicit instrument for keeping market exchange rates within the allowed margins of fluctuation. Three questions are posed: (i) Did EMS central banks "lean against the wind"? (ii) Did they sterilize foreign exchange interventions? (iii) Were foreign exchange interventions effective to counter exchange rate trends?

Interest rate shocks are an additional instrument often used by monetary authorities in attempts to lessen exchange market pressures. In chapter 4, we assess the ability of EMS central banks to influence exchange rates and international reserves by resorting to the management of market interest rates.

It is often argued that the EMS is an asymmetric exchange rate regime in which Germany provides the monetary anchor for the remaining participants. Whether the monetary policies adopted by non-Germany countries have, in practice, been dependent on a German standard is the focus of chapter 5. We suggest a technique that analyzes the extent to which EMS central banks used the domestic credit component of high-powered money as a policy instrument for achieving internal targets.

The EMS discipline or credibility hypothesis emerged as an explanation of why inflation-prone countries decided to participate in the EMS. The validity of the discipline hypothesis is questioned in chapter 6. Most of the previous empirical work in this field did not approach the issue in an appropriate manner, in the sense that the analyses focused only on inflation. The methodology used in chapter 6 focuses on all the variables included in the EMS discipline hypothesis, i.e. money, exchange rates, output, and inflation, and investigates whether the EMS has been operating as an arrangement that, through self-imposed discipline, weakened the incentives for monetary expansions.

According to some observers, the credibility of EMS central parities has improved over time. In chapter 7, statistical searches for such improvements are reported. In order to detect potential shifts in credibility, the analysis focuses on the behavior of the systematic component of forward excess returns.

CHAPTER 2
The origins, design and working of the European Monetary System

The purpose of this chapter is to provide some background for the chapters below where a critical assessment of the working of the EMS is undertaken. We start with a brief historical note on the route leading to the EMS and continue with a brief description of the main elements in the design of the system. The chapter is closed with a brief reference to the realignments of the system and foreign exchange interventions by EMS central banks.[2]

2.1. The origins of the EMS

The members of the EEC enjoyed exchange rate stability for many years as a result of the working of the Bretton Woods exchange system. However, at the beginning of the 1970s, the international monetary system underwent drastic transformation, and the system of fixed exchange rates was abandoned. The wide fluctuations of exchange rates that followed the breakdown of the Bretton Woods regime were perceived as a danger to European economic integration. This concern led the EEC countries to devise a mechanism that could stabilize the members' exchange rates.

In order to limit the variability of exchange rates, the first arrangement among European central banks was the so-called *"Snake in the Tunnel"* started in April 1972. This arrangement was an answer to the Smithsonian Agreement that increased the margins of fluctuation of the dollar exchange rates to ±2.25. These new bands of the collapsing Bretton Woods regime would mean, in practice, that European exchange rates could move within a band of 9 percent. This was deemed

[2]Those readers interested in a detailed chronology of the making and working of the European Monetary System and of the previous European monetary arrangements can resort to Gros and Thygesen (1992), chapters 1-3, and the references therein. Detailed descriptions of the design of the EMS can be found in, for example, Commission of the European Communities (1979) and Van Ypersele (1985). See also Ungerer *et al.* (1983; 1986; 1990) for successive updating of the developments in the EMS. The official texts containing the resolutions which gave rise to the European Monetary System can be found in Commission of the European Communities (1979).

to be too wide a margin of fluctuation for the Common Market exchange rates and it was decided to limit the margins for the EEC bilateral parities to ±2.25.

The *"Snake in the Tunnel"* did not have a long life. In March 1973, the European central banks decided to stop defending the parities of their currencies with the dollar. The *"tunnel"* was thus abandoned and only the *"Snake"* (with the same margins of ±2.25 percent) was kept alive. In spite of some turbulances, the *"Snake"* lasted until 1979, but France and Italy left the arrangement in the early 1970s. Ireland and the U.K. were members for less than two months in 1972. Sweden and Norway, which were not members of the EEC, joined the *"Snake"* in March 1973 but the Swedish krona left in 1977, while the Norwegian krone stayed until the dismantling of the arrangement two years later.

The *"Snake"* was not considered the best device for limiting European exchange rate fluctuations for two main reasons. First, not all EEC countries were permanent members of the system. The second reason has to do with the asymmetry of exchange market intervention. Although the participating countries had the obligation to intervene when their respective currencies reached the bilateral margins, in practice the adjustment was made through the weak-currency country's loss of international reserves.

In order to overcome these drawbacks of the *"Snake"*, a new exchange arrangement was designed. The *European Monetary System* was formally launched on March 13, 1979. All countries belonging to the EEC became automatically members of the EMS. However, not all adhered to the Exchange Rate Mechanism (ERM), the main element of the EMS.[3] Among the founding countries, the United Kingdom was the only EEC country that decided to remain outside the ERM. The U.K. started full participation in the EMS in October 1990 but left the ERM in September 1992. The Italian lira abandoned the ERM also in September 1992. Among the countries that joined the EEC after 1979, i.e., Greece, Portugal, and Spain, only Greece remains out of the ERM. Spain started full participation in the EMS in June 1989 and Portugal in April 1992.

The objective of the EMS was formally stated as the achievement of a zone of monetary stability in Europe. In practice the system consists of a multilateral agreement to manage exchange rates as summarized below.

2.2. The design of the EMS

Among the elements of the system established in 1979 is the European Currency Unit (ECU), a monetary unit composed of a basket of Community currencies. The new European currency unit replaced the existing European Unit of Account that was primarily used as a common denominator in EEC budgets and as a reference value to set the prices under the Common Agricultural Policy. To the ECU was assigned, among others, the *numeraire* role for fixing the central parities. For that matter, the ECU took the role of the U.S. dollar in the previous European exchange arrangements.

[3] Such that the ERM is often termed EMS.

All currencies of EEC countries have an ECU-related fixed exchange rate expressed in a certain quantity of currency per ECU. Crossing these ECU central rates, a series of bilateral central parities are obtained for each EEC currency. The market exchange rates of the currencies fully participating in the EMS are allowed to float, within some limits, around these bilateral central parities.

The margins of fluctuation were set at ±2.25 percent but the countries which were not in the *"Snake"* at the time of the formation of the EMS could opt for a margin of ±6.0 percent. Only Italy adopted this wider band and kept it until January 1990, when she decided to join the narrower one. The U.K., Spain and Portugal also joined the ERM with a ±6.0 percent band. The U.K. kept the wide band during his two years of membership while the other newcomers kept it until August 1993 when the EMS was practically dismantled through the general adoption of a ±15.0 percent band (the only exception being the Dutch guilder/Deutsche mark exchange rate which kept the original narrow band of ±2.25 percent).

According to the rules of the ERM, the exchange rate bands should be defended through interventions in the foreign exchange market. Only as a last resort and under nonsustainable conditions would negotiations between the member countries eventually lead to realignments in the central parities. These require common agreement of all ERM participants and the Commission of the European Communities.

The design of the ERM comprises compulsory interventions at the margins, as in the *"Snake"*, and intra-marginal interventions. The latter type of intervention was thought to give the EMS the symmetry not provided by the previous European exchange rate systems.

As in the *"Snake"*, intervention is compulsory when two currencies reach the limits of fluctuation in relation to each other. The two central banks have to intervene in order to keep the market exchange rate within the band. The issuing bank of the strong currency purchases the weak currency. Conversely, the central bank of the weak currency sells the strong currency. In theory, interventions at the margins may be unlimited given that the maximum limits of fluctuation are known to the public and, at those prices, central banks are forced to satisfy all market demand and supply.

Besides the compulsory interventions at the margins, ERM central banks can also carry out intra-marginal interventions on the basis of the *divergence indicator*. The divergence indicator allows the positioning of the exchange rate of any EMS currency against the Community weighted average (ECU) and, thereby, identifies the currencies deviating from that average. The divergence indicator for each currency shows how much the ECU market rate is deviating from the ECU central rate.

When the ECU market rate of a given currency appreciates or depreciates by 75 percent of the maximum allowed spread, the currency is said to have reached the *divergence threshold*. Crossing the divergence threshold presumes, but does not force, the country issuing the diverging currency to take action in attempts to drive the market exchange rate towards the ECU central rate. Among these actions are again interventions in the exchange market. In contrast to interventions at the margin, intra-marginal interventions are carried out by only one country.

The divergence indicator was an innovation brought forth by the EMS and was designed to give symmetry to the system.[4] The responsibility for taking action would lie with the weak-currency countries or with the strong-currency countries, depending on which one was deviating from the partners. The bias of the *"Snake"* towards the policy stance of the low-inflation countries was supposed to be smoothed by the operation of the divergence indicator. This new element was thought to work in an automatic way and favour the policy stance adopted by the majority of the member countries.

Apart from intra-marginal interventions based on the divergence indicator, the design of the EMS allows for optional intra-marginal interventions initiated by any central bank. Since interventions at the margin may incur the risk of requiring hudge amounts of international reserves, the optional intra-marginal intervention was thought to slowdown the tendency for a currency to approach the margin.

Through the *very short term financing* (VSTF) mechanism, the EMS provides credit facilities for carrying out foreign exchange interventions. The VSTF consists of credit lines among the central banks participating in the ERM. Since interventions at the margin are compulsory, it was decided that the use of the credit lines for this type of interventions is automatic and the amounts are unlimited. The renewal of a given credit is, however, only partial - according to the original design of the EMS, a credit matures in one and a half month's time.

For intra-marginal interventions the VSTF is not automatic. Furthermore, intra-marginal interventions with ERM currencies are subject to authorization by the central bank whose currency is to be bought or sold.

With the Basel/Nyborg agreement in September 1987, the use of the VSTF was extended, under certain conditions, to intra-marginal intervention operations. Nevertheless, the access to the credit lines for that purpose did not become automatic. The Basel/Nyborg agreement also extended to two and half months the maturity of VSTF for marginal interventions while the amounts of credit renewals were increased as well.

Besides VSTF, the original design of the EMS contains two additional credit mechanisms: the *short term monetary support* (STMS) and the *medium term financial support* (MTFS). Both credit lines were created to support the financing of balance of payments deficits, the former for temporary needs and the latter for longer term difficulties.

The European Monetary Cooperation Fund was appointed to monitor the EMS and to administer the credit facilities. These had been the functions of the Fund since April 1973, when it was set up to supervise the *"Snake"*.

2.3. The working of the EMS

In a description of the motivations both for the need to replace the *"Snake"* by another exchange rate arrangement and for the design chosen for the EMS, the

[4]Some technical limitations of the divergence indicator are pointed out in Salop (1981).

Commission of the European Communities (1979) emphasizes the importance and role of the divergence indicator as follows:

> *Some countries took the view that the earlier exchange rate scheme* (i.e., the "Snake") *was not only lacking in symmetry and tended to produce an alignment of all the participating currencies on the German mark but also contained other shortcomings which helped to explain why three Community currencies withdrew from it in succession:*
>
> *(i) in spite of more extensive recourse to discretionary intra-marginal intervention by participating countries, there was no institutional means of preventing the emergence of strains or of taking action before currencies reached their 2,25% margins, thereby triggering compulsory and, in theory, unlimited intervention;*
>
> *(ii) apart from the very short-term financing facilities, the system did not possess sufficient resources to cope with large bouts of speculation caused either by domestic strains or by the weakness of non-member currencies and the emergence of the German mark as a 'safe haven' currency;*
>
> ....
>
> *The major innovations in the EMS took shape as these problems were tackled and as the negotiations progressed. ... These innovations, which made the system quite different from the snake and account for its originality, are as follows:*
>
> *(i) introduction of the ECU in the Community exchange rate scheme, and its role in fixing exchange rates, thereby making it possible, among other things to identify the currency which is tending to diverge from the others (principle of the divergence indicator);*
>
> *(ii) the divergence indicator, which is designed to prevent strains appearing in the system by providing, for the first time, an objective basis on which to trigger consultations and by introducing, before the bilateral limits are reached, a 'presumption to act', i.e. to make adjustments, on the part of the different countries;*[5]

Despite being advertised as the main innovation of the EMS, the divergence indicator never worked and the operation of the system launched in 1979 became, in practice, very similar to its predecessor. Two main reasons are usually pointed out for the inoperation of the divergence indicator. One is that the Bundesbank was not willing to adjust to the monetary policies of those partners with a history of higher inflation rates. The Bundesbank actually opposed the formation of the EMS but had to accept it, since participation in international exchange rate arrangements is, according to German law, a decision of the government.[6] The second reason is related to the former one. In fact, it seems that some of Germany's partners in the EMS were interested in changing their performances in terms of inflation and,

[5]Quoted from Commission of the European Communities(1979), pages 71-72.

[6]See von Hagen (1989; 1993) and Neumann and von Hagen (1993).

therefore, were not interested in the working of a mechanism allowing them to follow autonomous policies.[7]

Table 2.1 lists the realignments that the EMS underwent until August 1993, when the bands were widened to ±15 percent. The table shows that the German mark has observed a systematic tendency to appreciate relative to the remaining currencies so that it is the only currency in the system that has never devalued. This has a straightforward interpretation: German monetary policy was the one that systematically diverged from the average policy of the EMS. If the divergence indicator had worked, there would have been massive intra-marginal foreign exchange interventions by the Bundesbank and many of the observed realignments would have been avoided. The data for foreign exchange interventions in the EMS reflect, however, a very different reality. Table 2.2 shows how much of the interventions carried out with ERM currencies were of the marginal and intra-marginal types and shows the respective shares of the Bundesbank and of the set of the remaining central banks in the system.[8]

Table 2.2 shows that the Bundesbank never intervened within the margins. This is the clearest evidence that the divergence indicator never performed the rôle devised by the founders of the EMS. Furthermore, on the whole, German interventions in the EMS have been negligible after 1982 and the conclusion that can be drawn from the table is that the responsibility of defending EMS exchange rates had been assigned, in practice, to the remaining central banks in the system. Whether interventions in foreign exchange markets have been an effective way to stabilize EMS exchange rates is the question addressed in chapter 3.

Another observation that can be made on Table 2.2 is that intra-marginal interventions have been relatively heavier after 1987. This might be related to the dismantling of most of the exchange controls that was observed in this period. Without such controls, there is an increase in the likelihood of speculative attacks, if market exchange rates are at the limit of the bands.

The frequency of realignments in the EMS has been used as a criterion to describe the working of the system. Between March 1979 and September 1992, three sub-periods are usually identified. As reported in Table 2.1, the frequency of realignments was quite high until March 1983. Between March 1983 and January 1987, only three realignments were undertaken. Since then we have observed a period of more than five years where the only realignment was a technical one to narrow the bands of the Italian lira from ±6 to ±2.25 percent. Gros and Thygesen (1992) label these three sub-periods as "a turbulent start", "a calmer intermediate phase" and "an EMS without realignments", respectively. In 1990, with a period of more than three calm years, the European arrangement of exchange rates was even named "New EMS" [see Giavazzi and Spaventa (1990)], meaning an EMS with central exchange rates accepted by the market in a credible way. If this had

[7]The issue of the anti-inflationary role of the EMS is investigated in chapter 6 below.

[8]Table 2.2 does not include intervention carried out with dollars. Intervention with dollars is consistent both with the purpose of affecting the dollar market and the purpose of affecting EMS exchange rates. For the periods reported in Table 2.2, foreign exchange intervention carried out by all ERM central banks with dollars has steadly fallen from 139.4 billion (of which 25.4 billion are from the Bundesbank) in 1979-82 to 29.5 billion (of which 12.4 billion are from the Bundesbank) in 1988-89. See Gros and Thygesen (1992), Table 4.5.1.

not been the case it wouldn't have been possible to observe stability in foreign exchange markets free from capital mobility restrictions. The turbulances were, however, to come.

Table 2.1 - Realignments in the EMS (% changes), 1979:3-1993:8

Date	BF	DK	DM	FF	IP	LIT	HFL	GBP	PTE	ESP
24-09-79	-	+2.9	-2.0	-	-	-	-	-	-	-
30-11-79	-	+4.8	-	-	-	-	-	-	-	-
23-03-81	-	-	-	-	-	+6.0	-	-	-	-
05-10-81	-	-	-5.5	+3.0	-	+3.0	-5.5	-	-	-
22-02-82	+8.5	+3.0	-	-	-	-	-	-	-	-
14-06-82	-	-	-4 1/4	+5 3/4	-	+2 3/4	-4 1/4	-	-	-
21-03-83	-1.5	-2.5	-5.5	+2.5	+3.5	+2.5	-3.5	-	-	-
22-07-85	-2.0	-2.0	-2.0	-2.0	-2.0	+6.0	-2.0	-	-	-
07-04-86	-1.0	-1.0	-3.0	+3.0	-	-	-3.0	-	-	-
04-08-86	-	-	-	-	+8.0	-	-	-	-	-
12-01-87	-2.0	-	-3.0	-	-	-	-3.0	-	-	-
08-01-90*	-	-	-	-	-	+3.7	-	-	-	-
13-09-92	-3.5	-3.5	-3.5	-3.5	-3.5	+3.5	-3.5	-3.5	-3.5	-3.5
16-09-92	-	-	-	-	-	-	-	Susp	-	-
17-09-92	-	-	-	-	-	Susp	-	-	-	+5.0
21-11-92	-	-	-	-	-	-	-	-	+6.0	+6.0
30-01-93	-	-	-	-	+10	-	-	-	-	-
13-05-93	-	-	-	-	-	-	-	-	+6.5	+8.0

Notes:

1) BF-Belgian franc; DK-Danish krone; DM-Deutsche mark; FF-French franc; IP-Irish punt; LIT-Italian lira; HFL-Dutch guilder; GBP-British pound; PTE-Portuguese escudo; ESP-Spanish peseta.

2) A revaluation is denoted with a "-" sign while "+" denotes devaluation.

*At this time, the margin of fluctuation of the Italian lira was narrowed from ±6% to ±2.25%. This narrowing was done in such way as to leave the upper limit of the band unchanged.

Source: European Economy - Supplement A (various issues).

Table 2.2 - Foreign exchange interventions by EMS central banks (%)

	1979-82	1983-85	1986-87	1988-89
Bundesbank				
• at the margin	16.2	2.7	2.4	0.0
• intramarginal	0.0	0.0	0.0	0.0
Remaining central banks				
• at the margin	35.0	21.4	14.0	2.7
• intramarginal	58.8	75.9	83.6	97.3
Total	100.0	100.0	100.0	100.0

Source: Computed from Gros and Thygesen (1992), Table 4.5.1.

CHAPTER 3
"Leaning against the wind" in the EMS: Did it work? An analysis of the period from 1979 to 1988

3.1. Introduction

According to the design of the ERM, interventions in the foreign exchange market are the only explicit instrument for keeping the market exchange rates within the allowed margins of fluctuation. The EMS was, however, subject to eleven realignments in its first eight years of life. This questions the ability of interventions to affect market exchange rates.

This chapter provides a detailed analysis of foreign exchange market intervention policy in the first decade of the EMS. This is done by answering the three questions listed and discussed below:

(i) How did ERM central banks react to changes in market exchange rates?

At the theoretical level, there are three possible answers to this question. One is that central banks simply did not react. This would imply that changes in the market exchange rate did not lead to any intervention in the exchange market and that the EMS worked like a floating exchange rate regime.

An alternative policy would be for the monetary authorities to attempt to speed up exchange rate adjustments by buying domestic currency when it is appreciating or selling when it is depreciating. As shown by Roper and Turnovsky (1980), this might be an optimal intervention policy if the authorities want to achieve an exchange rate target associated with, for example, employment objectives.

Given the design of the ERM, the two alternatives above are unlikely. In particular, the second type of exchange rate policy would not be consistent with a cooperative exchange rate regime, like the EMS.

A third alternative for the ERM central banks is to counter movements in the exchange rates by intervening in the foreign exchange market. In accordance with the rules of the ERM, this "leaning-against-the-wind" behavior would be the most likely.

Besides the direction of intervention, a related and important aspect is the strength of the central banks' reaction. The degree of the reaction to changes in the market exchange rate determines the (lack of) stability of the stock of international reserves held by the central bank and might determine the effectiveness of intervention.

(ii) Did ERM central banks sterilize foreign exchange market intervention?

When a central bank intervenes in the foreign exchange market, the foreign component of the monetary base is altered, while - depending on the behavior of the monetary authorities in the domestic money market - the domestic component may or may not be changed.

When the domestic-currency counterpart of the change in the central bank's stock of international reserves is offset by a change of the same magnitude but the opposite sign in the domestic credit component, the aggregate monetary base is not changed. This situation is often referred to as "sterilized foreign exchange intervention". The central bank sterilizes foreign exchange market operations by simultaneously intervening in the domestic money market. For example, an official purchase of foreign currency can be sterilized through a corresponding open-market sale of domestic bonds. By means of this operation, foreign exchange market intervention amounts to a swap of foreign reserves for domestic assets and is divorced from monetary policy. With sterilized intervention central banks try to control the supply of money while pegging the exchange rate.

Non-sterilized intervention occurs whenever the change in the domestic credit component of the base does not fully offset the domestic currency counterpart of the change in foreign reserves. In this case, intervention in foreign exchange markets leads to a change in the money stock.

This distinction between sterilized and non-sterilized intervention is important since it might provide an answer to the next question.

(iii) Did interventions by ERM central banks affect the path of market exchange rates?

It is generally agreed that, in the medium and long run, the exchange rate reflects differentials in money growth adjusted for output growth differentials. Accordingly, if ERM central banks do not sterilize the changes in foreign reserves resulting from exchange market intervention with offsetting operations in the domestic money market, one may expect - given the ensuing change in money stock - the exchange rate to be affected sooner or later. However, if intervention in the foreign exchange market leaves the money stock unaltered, one should not immediately conclude that the market exchange rate is not affected. In fact, it has been hypothesized that there are two ways through which sterilized intervention might be effective in driving the exchange rate. One alternative is based on the portfolio holding balance and the other on the signalling that intervention may convey.[9]

[9]For surveys on the effectiveness of sterilized intervention, see Genberg (1981), Obstfeld (1982), Kenen (1987), Bordo and Schwartz (1990), and Almekinders and Eijffinger (1991).

While leaving the monetary base unchanged, sterilized intervention alters the relative supply of domestic and foreign assets. This may give rise to unbalanced private portfolios if, due to the existence of nondiversifiable risk, domestic and foreign assets are not perfect substitutes in international portfolios. Sterilized intervention would operate effectively, if the re-establishment of portfolio balance between domestic and foreign assets requires the relative prices of the denominating currencies to be altered.[10]

The signal that exchange market interventions convey is another channel through which sterilized intervention may be effective. The argument, advanced by Mussa (1981), is that intervention may be used by central banks to release credible information to the public about future monetary policy. The private sector's response to the signal then drives the exchange rate in the direction desired by the monetary authorities.[11] The credibility of the signal results from the reputational costs associated with false signals. These costs are the loss both of reputation and of international reserves resulting from interventions in the "wrong" direction.

If neither one of these two channels operates in practice, that is, if sterilized intervention is unable to counter exchange rate trends, we would expect ERM interventions to be of the non-sterilized type. Otherwise, there would be a systematic change in the stock of international reserves, unless the monetary authorities have some other instrument (e.g., interest rate management), to counter exchange rate movements. If the leaning-against-the-wind-cum-sterilization leads to undesirable cumulative changes in foreign reserves and, at the same time, monetary authorities do not have any other alternative instrument to affect the exchange rate, a realignment in the central parities is an inevitable outcome.

To answer the above questions we propose and apply in this chapter an empirical model that charaterizes the intervention policies adopted by the ERM central banks during the period of frequent realignments. As explained below, the analysis relates to changes of exchange rates within the bands. The focus is on the intra-European Deutsche mark (DM) exchange markets. Despite the fact that the designers of the EMS did not designate a special role for any member currency, the DM became the *de facto* reference currency for pegging within the EMS.

The remaining part of this chapter is organized as follows. Section 3.2 describes the actual working of the intra-European DM exchange markets, using a theoretical model of exchange market pressure (EMP) of the type suggested by Girton and Roper (1977). In section 3.3 we suggest an empirical model for simultaneously assessing the strength of the "leaning against the wind" and sterilization policies and the effectiveness of intervention. The data are described in section 3.4 and the results presented in section 3.5. Finally, section 3.6 contains a summary and conclusions.

---

[10]For an application of the portfolio effect of foreign exchange intervention, see Dominguez and Frankel (1990; 1993).

[11]For an application of the expectations effect of foreign exchange intervention, see Dominguez (1986). See also Dominguez and Frankel (1990).

3.2. An exchange market pressure model of the EMS

The equilibrium in the European DM exchange markets can be described by the relationship between the German money market and the money markets of Germany's partners in the ERM. Consider the following three equations of the monetary sector for any ERM member country, say, country j:[12]

$$M_j^d = P_j\, Y_j^{\beta_j}\, e^{-\alpha_j i_j} \tag{3.1}$$

$$M_j^s = a_j\, MB_j \equiv a_j\, (DC_j + FR_j) \tag{3.2}$$

$$M_j^d = M_j^s \tag{3.3}$$

where

$M^d{}_j$	=nominal money demand
P_j	=price level
Y_j	=real income
i_j	=opportunity cost of holding money (e.g., nominal interest rate)
β_j	=income elasticity of demand for money
α_j	=interest rate semi-elasticity of demand for money
$M^s{}_j$	=nominal money supply
a_j	=money multiplier
MB_j	=monetary base
DC_j	=domestic component of monetary base
FR_j	=foreign component of monetary base

Equation (3.1) is the usual exponential specification of the money demand function. Equation (3.2) states that the money supply is equal to the product of the monetary base and the money multiplier, a_j. The monetary base can be decomposed into the domestic and the foreign components, DC_j and FR_j, respectively. The money market equilibrium condition is expressed by equation (3.3).

The foreign component of the monetary base is obtained through the accumulation of international reserve flows, evaluated at the exchange rate prevailing at the time of the relevant transaction. Such a procedure for obtaining FR_j prevents capital gains or losses in the stock of foreign reserves from affecting the monetary base.

The combination of equations (3.1)-(3.3) yields

$$a_j\, MB_j = a_j\, (DC_j + FR_j) = P_j\, Y_j^{\beta_j}\, e^{-\alpha_j i_j} \tag{3.4}$$

[12] The model is not EMS specific and applies to any exchange rate regime.

Rewriting the equalities in (3.4) in percentage changes of the variables over time and assuming, for simplicity, a constant money multiplier, yields

$$mb_j = dc_j + fr_j = \pi_j + \beta_j\, y_j - \alpha_j\, i_j^{'} \tag{3.5}$$

where mb, π, and y are the percentage counterparts of MB, P, and Y, respectively; i_j' is the time derivative of the nominal interest rate, while dc and fr are the changes in DC and FR in a given time period, relative to the monetary base (MB) in the beginning of that period.[13]

The assumption of relative purchasing power parity (PPP) between Germany (Ger) and any other member of the ERM, say country j, implies that

$$s_j = \pi_j - \pi_{Ger} \tag{3.6}$$

where s_j is the rate of depreciation of currency j in terms of the Deutsche mark.[14] The money market equilibrium conditions, for both Germany and country j, lead to[15]

$$s_j - fr_j + fr_{Ger} = dc_j - dc_{Ger} - \beta\,(y_j - y_{Ger}) + \alpha\,(i_j - i_{Ger})^{'} \tag{3.7}$$

where the income elasticity and the interest rate semi-elasticity of demand for money are assumed, for simplicity, to be the same for both countries, i.e., $\beta=\beta_j=\beta_{Ger}$ and $\alpha=\alpha_j=\alpha_{Ger}$.

Between two consecutive realignments in central parities, the equilibrium in the European DM exchange markets can be achieved in seven alternative ways. These alternatives can be derived from combinations of the variables on the left-hand side of equation (3.7):

(i) keep exchange rates perfectly fixed and let only Germany's central bank intervene ($s_j=fr_j=0$ while $fr_{Ger}\neq 0$);

(ii) keep exchange rates perfectly fixed and let only country j's central bank intervene ($s_j=fr_{Ger}=0$ while $fr_j\neq 0$);

(iii) keep exchange rates perfectly fixed and let both Germany's and its ERM partner's central banks intervene ($s_j=0$ while $fr_j\neq 0$ and $fr_{Ger}\neq 0$);

[13]The derivation of (3.5) can be found in Blejer (1977).

[14]The use of relative PPP instead of its absolute version is required here because expression (3.4) has been previously differentiated. There is at least one reason for this common practice. Since figures for the variable DC are not available in general, it is convenient in empirical work to use dc, which can be obtained in a residual way (see the data appendix at the end of this chapter).

[15]PPP does not necessarily have to hold. It is enough to assume that deviations from PPP are a linear function of income, interest rates, and money stocks (or a subset of these variables) for relation (3.7) to hold.

(iv) allow exchange rates to float freely while both central banks refrain from intervention ($fr_j=fr_{Ger}=0$ while $s_j \neq 0$);

(v) let exchange rates float in a managed way by letting Germany's central bank unilaterally defend the margins of fluctuation ($fr_j=0$ while $s_j \neq 0$ and $fr_{Ger} \neq 0$);

(vi) let exchange rates float in a managed way by letting country j's central bank unilaterally defend the margins ($fr_{Ger}=0$ while $s_j \neq 0$ and $fr_j \neq 0$);

(vii) let exchange rates float in a managed way by letting both Germany's and its ERM partner's central banks defend the margins ($s_j \neq 0$, $fr_j \neq 0$ and $fr_{Ger} \neq 0$).

As noted in the preceding chapter, the Deutsche mark is, within the EMS, the currency that deviated the most from the system's average. According to the rules of the divergence indicator, one would, therefore, expect the Bundesbank to have made frequent intra-marginal intervention. We have seen, however, that Germany never took part in intra-marginal operations. Given that intra-marginal intervention has been the most frequently applied type of intervention (see Table 2.2), the responsibility of keeping the DM exchange rates within the bands seems to have been left to the non-German ERM members. On the basis of this intervention pattern, equilibrium in the European DM exchange markets has been achieved mainly through alternative (vi): exchange rates were allowed to move within the margins of fluctuation which were defended by non-German ERM partners. This may have been part of a tacit agreement among the participating central banks: the Bundesbank would worry about the U.S. dollar exchange rate and the other ERM members about the intra ERM exchange rates. Such a behavior is acknowledged by the Commission of the European Communities (1990) which notes that "*most of the intra-marginal intervention was carried out by partner countries while the 'centre'* [Germany] *played the role of 'representing' the whole system vis-à-vis the rest of the world.*"[16]

On the basis of this discussion, equation (3.7) can be rewritten by moving fr_{Ger} to the right-hand side and merging it with dc_{Ger} to get a single variable, mb_{Ger}. Instead of confining the German monetary aggregate to be the monetary base, we reintroduce the German money multiplier in the new equation which becomes

$$s_j - fr_j = dc_j - m_{Ger} - \beta\,(y_j - y_{Ger}) + \alpha\,(i_j - i_{Ger})' \tag{3.8}$$

where m_{Ger} is the percentage change in the German money stock. Equation (3.8) says that changes in the j/DM exchange rate fundamentals (i.e., the right-hand side of the equation) are reflected in the j/DM exchange rate and/or in the stock of foreign reserves of country j.

Equation (3.8) provides a formal description of how equilibrium in the European DM exchange markets has been achieved. Since the bands of the EMS did not

[16] Quoted from Commission of the European Communities (1990), page 182.

allow the DM exchange rate to fully absorb market pressures, and given that the DM was the strongest currency in the system, equilibrium in the exchange market was achieved through losses of international reserves in the weak currency countries. These losses could be periodically recovered through realignments in the central parities. Rebuilding the stock of foreign reserves required realignments that left the devaluating currency strong right after the shift in the bands. As noted by von Hagen (1989), this has actually been the case in most of EMS realignments and was also in the interest of Germany. Since most of the Bundesbank's foreign exchange intervention in the EMS was in support of weak currencies around realignments, a weak DM just after its revaluation would imply that foreign exchange intervention had no lasting effect on the German money supply. The initial monetary expansion resulting from the increase in the stock of foreign reserves was reversed right after the realignments.

3.3. Assessing foreign exchange intervention: Methodology

A thorough analysis of foreign exchange intervention policy in the EMS requires the examination of how the variables s_j, fr_j and dc_j, defined above, interact when there is a change in the market exchange rate.

The literature has focused on different pairs of the three variables:

(i) The link between dc and fr has been used to assess whether a country follows an autonomous monetary policy or whether instead, monetary autonomy is lost due to exchange rate pegging. It is postulated that, in an equation where dc is the dependent variable, a coefficient for fr (the so-called *sterilization coefficient*) equal to -1 means that monetary authorities are exclusively commited to obtaining certain domestic objectives. On the contrary, the more the sterilization coefficient approaches zero - that is, the less the changes in the foreign component of monetary base are offset by changes in the domestic component of the monetary base - the more the domestic objectives are sacrificed to the external constraint.[17]

(ii) The relationship between dc and fr has also been analyzed in the opposite direction. In the context of fixed exchange rate regimes, the variable fr has been taken as the dependent variable and the coefficient of dc, the so-called *offsetting coefficient*, has received a lot of attention. It is argued here that, in a fixed exchange rate regime, monetary authorities, although able to control the composition of the monetary base, are not able to control the magnitude of the aggregate. This being the case, any change in dc would be offset by a change of fr of the same magnitude but opposite

[17]For empirical estimations of sterilization equations see, for example, Herring and Marston (1977), Obstfeld (1983), and Kearney and MacDonald (1986).

sign, implying a -1 coefficient for the domestic component of the monetary base.[18]

(iii) The offsetting coefficient has also been analyzed, as suggested by Girton and Roper (1977), in a broader manner. By merging the change in the exchange rate with that in the foreign component of the monetary base (giving rise to the so-called *exchange market pressure* variable), the estimation of the offsetting coefficient can be extended to periods covering both the polar regimes of fixed and freely floating exchange rates as well as managed float. In contrast to (ii), where the offsetting operation is made only via foreign reserves, the exchange market pressure variable allows changes in dc to fall upon fr and/or s, depending on the actual exchange rate regime.[19]

(iv) The offsetting coefficient based on the hybrid exchange market pressure measure mentioned in (iii) does not say anything about where the pressures are falling. Under a managed float, where the pressure is born by both foreign reserves and the exchange rate, the *leaning-against-the-wind* coefficient is used to measure the way this pressure is shared between the two variables. It is, then, not surprising that attention has also been directed in many studies to the coefficient of s in regressions where fr is the dependent variable.[20]

In order to answer the three questions raised in the introduction to this chapter, we suggest an approach that considers the interactions between all three variables, s, fr, and dc, simultaneously. Our approach thus differs from the partial approaches discussed above. By focusing on the effects that follow a shock in the market exchange rate, we are able to assess the direction and magnitude of central banks interventions and whether or not the interventions are sterilized. We are also in a position to assess the ability of the central banks to affect the market exchange rate through those operations.

If the central banks react to changes in exchange rates by intervening in the foreign exchange market, Friedman's "long and variable lag" is likely to apply, that is, the achievement of a long-run equilibrium, represented by expression (3.8), might take time to realize. Although many hypothetical situations could be

---

[18]Offsetting coefficients were estimated by, among others, Kouri and Porter (1974) and Kamas (1986).

[19]The offseting coefficient based on the exchange-market-pressure variable was estimated by Girton and Roper (1977) for the $Canadian/$US market and was more recently re-estimated by Burdekin and Burkett (1990) for the same market. The estimations were implemented in an econometric model of the type described by expression (3.8), with the two variables on the left-hand side merged into a single variable. Hodgson and Schneck (1981) also applied a similar model to a set of developed countries.

[20]"Leaning-against-the-wind" reaction functions were estimated by, for example, Artus (1976), Quirk (1977), Branson *et al.* (1977;1979), Longworth (1980), Kearney and MacDonald (1986), and Gärtner (1987).

presented in support of this, we confine ourselves to three examples that seem quite realistic. The long-run equilibrium takes time to materialize if, for example,

- the monetary authorities are willing to sterilize foreign exchange market interventions but the participants in the money markets are only willing (or able) to participate in the transactions at a slow pace;

- central bank interventions are not sterilized but the public observes the figures of the ensuing change in the money stock with a lag and, thereby, the trend of the market exchange rate is inverted only some time after the initial interventions;

-interventions are followed by sterilization which prevents the adjustment of domestic interest rates and, thereby, movements in international reserves continue for some time.[21]

Whatever approach is adopted to analyze intervention in the exchange market, the three situations above illustrate the need for the incorporation of dynamics in the analysis. This need is empirically shown by von Hagen (1989), who takes this problem into account and reverses previous empirical results on German intervention/sterilization policies.

Bearing in mind that the inter-relationships between the variables of interest are such that a change in any one may have important indirect impacts on others (partly due to endogenous policy responses) and that the full implications might take a time lag to realize, we suggest the use of a vector autoregression (VAR) model to analyze foreign exchange interventions in the DM markets of the EMS. This type of model allows for very general patterns of interaction among endogenous variables and is, therefore, appropriate for studying the transmission mechanisms.

Specifically, we estimate the joint process followed by the set of all variables involved in expression (3.8), except m_{Ger}, the relative change in the German money stock. The VAR estimation is thus for the relative change in the exchange rate (s_j), the change in the foreign component and in the domestic component of the monetary base relative to the monetary base stock (fr_j and dc_j, respectively), the income growth differential (y_j-y_{Ger}) and the change in the interest rate differential [$(i_j$-$i_{Ger})'$].

We assume that the German money stock is determined outside the model and is, therefore, taken as exogenous.[22] This assumption implies that neither German

---

[21]For the analysis of the trade-off, implicit in the choice of sterilization, between the control of the monetary base and that of international reserves, see Herring and Marston (1977).

[22]The imposition of the small country assumption also implies y_{Ger} and i_{Ger} to be determined outside the model. However, these two variables do not appear as separate variables in the model but are rather merged with the corresponding variables of the remaining ERM countries. By introducing the income and the interest rate differentials in the VARs, we assume that the two can both explain and be explained by s, fr, and dc. The use of the differentials aims at preserving degrees of freedom.

interventions in EMS exchange markets nor interventions by the remaining partners affect the money supply path in Germany. Given existing empirical evidence, the assumption seems a plausible one. For example, Fratianni and von Hagen (1990a) and MacDonald and Taylor (1991) report German monetary independence.[23] Mastropasqua, Micossi and Rinaldi (1988) report that Germany is the only EMS member that has been able to fully sterilize exchange market operations.[24] Although reversing previous conclusions regarding Bundesbank's sterilization operations, von Hagen (1989) also provides further evidence showing that EMS-related interventions did not have implications for the conduct of monetary policy in Germany.

Focusing on the non-deterministic component, the econometric model to be estimated is given by the vector autoregressive representation

$$A(L)\, x_t = u_t \qquad (3.9)$$

where

- $x_t \equiv \left[dc_j, fr_j, s_j, (i_j - i_{Ger}), (y_j - y_{Ger})\right]'$,
- $A(L) = \sum_{i=0}^{n} A_i L^i$ is a 5x5 matrix polynomial in the lag operator, (L),
- $A_0 = I$,
- The u's are the disturbances, representing that part of the dependent variable that is not predictable from knowledge of the lagged values of the regressors,
- $E\left(u_t\, u_t'\right) = \Sigma$, and
- $E\left(u_{it}\, u_{js}\right) = 0$ for $t \neq s$.

The autoregressive coefficients are usually difficult to interpret. In econometric applications, the best way of describing the distributed lag relations is to analyze the system's response to random shocks. This strategy, which is based on the moving average representation of the VAR model, is adopted in this study. Accordingly, once the reduced form (3.9) is estimated, it is inverted and each variable is expressed as a linear combination of its own current innovation and lagged innovations in all the variables in the system:

$$x_t = \left[A(L)\right]^{-1} u_t \qquad (3.10)$$

[23] German independence in the EMS does not mean dominance. See Fratianni and von Hagen (1990a;b;c;d).

[24] Earlier reports of German sterilization can be found in Artus (1976), Branson, Halttunen, and Masson (1977), Herring and Marston (1977), and Obstfeld (1983).

The innovations u_t are likely to be contemporaneously correlated. A generic representation of the contemporaneous model may be given by

$$\varepsilon_t = B\, u_t \tag{3.11}$$

such that $B\Sigma B'=\Pi$, where Π is a diagonal matrix and, therefore, $E(\varepsilon_{it}\varepsilon_{js})=0$, for all (t,s) and $i\neq j$.

In empirical work, a number of ways have been used to ensure the orthogonality of u_t. A popular method pioneered by Sims (1980a,b) is the recursive approach which assumes that the matrix B is lower triangular. In this method, the variables are ordered in such a way that an innovation in a given variable is assumed in the same period to only affect those variables that are lower in the list. The problem with this approach is that it is often difficult to find an appropriate economic interpretation for the coefficients. Furthermore, different orderings of variables can lead to different results.[25] In our study, we apply the simultaneous equations approach suggested by Blanchard and Watson (1984) and Bernanke (1986). This approach also imposes zero-type restrictions on the matrix B but does not necessarily require the assumption of a recursive structure. Although some degree of arbitrariness is incorporated, the degrees of freedom to orthogonalize the residuals are higher than in the recursive approach. The contemporaneous model for non-German ERM countries is specified as follows:

$$u_{dc_j} = \lambda_1\, u_{fr_j} + \lambda_2\, u_{(y_j - y_{Ger})} + \varepsilon_{dc_j} \tag{3.12.a}$$

$$u_{fr_j} = \lambda_3\, u_{s_j} + \varepsilon_{fr_j} \tag{3.12.b}$$

$$u_{s_j} = \lambda_4\, u_{(i_j - i_{Ger})'} + \varepsilon_{s_j} \tag{3.12.c}$$

$$u_{(i_j - i_{Ger})'} = \lambda_5\, u_{dc_j} + \varepsilon_{(i_j - i_{Ger})'} \tag{3.12.d}$$

$$u_{(y_j - y_{Ger})} = \varepsilon_{(y_j - y_{Ger})} \tag{3.12.e}$$

where the u's and the ε's stand for non-orthogonal and orthogonal innovations, respectively.[26,27]

---

[25] See Cooley and LeRoy (1985) and Spencer (1989).

[26] Since our model is overidentified (for identification we should impose only ten restrictions in the coefficients), the use of the term "orthogonal innovations" is somehow inappropriate.

[27] In the empirical work, we have tried alternative specifications to (3.12) but the results presented in this study (which is based on monthly data) are robust regardless of the adopted contemporaneous model. Due to the high correlations between the domestic and the foreign components of the monetary base, the results would be altered only if offsetting, instead of sterilization, is assumed to operate contemporaneously. The justification for choosing contemporaneous sterilization rather than contemporaneous offsetting is given below.

In the contemporaneous model above we allow for the possibility that the central bank intervenes in the foreign exchange market during the same period that changes in the exchange rate occur. The contemporaneous reaction of the central bank is given by λ_3 in equation (3.12.b). A positive λ_3 implies that the central bank "bends with the wind", while a negative one implies that the central bank "leans against the wind". We further allow for the possibility that, along with foreign exchange market intervention, the central bank also carries out offsetting operations in the money market. The contemporaneous sterilization coefficient is given by λ_1 in equation (3.12.a). The assumption that changes in the foreign component of the monetary base are contemporaneously offset by changes in the domestic credit component, and not the other way around, can be justified on two grounds. Since the central banks have permanent and updated information about the level of international reserves, they might immediately react in order to prevent a chosen path for the money supply to be affected by a change in foreign reserves. On the other hand, given that foreign exchange controls were adopted for many years by most countries in the ERM, it is not likely that an expansion in domestic credit leaks out, through international reserve flows, during a relatively short period.

A common target variable in sterilization equations is the deviation of the domestic income growth from its trend. The idea is to check whether monetary authorities respond to temporary fluctuations in output. In our VARs, we allow for the possibility that domestic monetary authorities react to the income fluctuations relative to German income. In the model, a negative λ_2 means that deviations in domestic income growth from German income growth are contemporaneously counteracted with domestic credit measures, while such deviations are supported, when λ_2 is positive.

The management of interest rates is often used as an alternative or even as a complement to foreign exchange intervention. The possibility that changes in nominal interest rates may contemporaneously affect the exchange rates is captured by equation (3.12.c). A negative (positive) λ_4 means that increases in the interest rate differentials lead to a contemporaneous appreciation (depreciation) of the intra-European DM exchange rates.

Equation (3.12.d) allows for the nominal interest rate differential to be contemporaneously affected by changes in domestic credit. In principle, ease in domestic credit would lead to a decrease in the interest rate differential and, therefore, to a negative λ_5. However, if such an increase is not accompanied by an increase in real income, it may result in devaluation expectations, leading to a positive λ_5.

Finally, it is assumed that the contemporaneous innovations in the income growth differential are exogenously determined. This is captured in equation (3.12.e).

Combining the contemporaneous model (3.11), or (3.12), with the moving average representation of the VAR model, expression (3.10), we obtain

$$x_t = C(L)\,\varepsilon_t \tag{3.13}$$

where

$$C(L) = [A(L)]^{-1} B^{-1} = \begin{bmatrix} c_{11}(L) & \cdots & c_{15}(L) \\ & \vdots & \\ c_{51}(L) & \cdots & c_{55}(L) \end{bmatrix} = \begin{bmatrix} \sum_{i=0}^{\infty} c_{11,i} L^i & \cdots & \sum_{i=0}^{\infty} c_{15,i} L^i \\ & \vdots & \\ \sum_{i=0}^{\infty} c_{51,i} L^i & \cdots & \sum_{i=0}^{\infty} c_{55,i} L^i \end{bmatrix}$$

and the subscripts attached to c correspond to the same order of the variables in vector x, i.e., $1=dc_j$, $2=fr_j$, $3=s_j$, $4=(i_j - i_{Ger})'$, $5=(y_j - y_{Ger})$.

In our methodology we follow the reasoning behind the standard analysis of the "leaning-against-the-wind" framework, that is, we assess the effects on foreign reserves resulting from an innovation in the exchange rate. However, the approach adopted in our work provides a deeper analysis in that the effects are assessed in a dynamic way. Furthermore, the analysis is not restricted to the effects on the foreign reserves but also covers the effects on the remaining endogenous variables in the system and thus allows us to assess sterilization and the effectiveness of foreign exchange market intervention.

The analysis is based on impulse response functions. These functions trace the responses of the ith element of x_{t+n} to innovations in the jth variable at date t, with n=0,1,2,... . Our focus is on the effects on foreign reserves (fr_j), domestic credit (dc_j), and exchange rate (s_j) resulting from a unit one-shot shock in the exchange rate. Referring to expression (3.13), the dynamic responses of these three variables are given by $c_{23}(1)$, $c_{13}(1)$, and $c_{33}(1)$, respectively.

3.4. Data

The DM exchange markets under investigation are those of the founding countries of the ERM, i.e., Belgium, Denmark, France, Italy, and the Netherlands.[28] We use monthly data for the period beginning in March 1979 to June 1988 for all countries in question, except France whose data set ends in October 1987.[29,30] The period chosen covers all the realignments that the European Monetary System underwent before enjoying the stability of five and half years preceding the crisis initiated in September 1992.

The variables included in the VARs are those of the exchange market pressure model described in section 3.2. and are, thus, in first differences. For convenience,

---

[28] Ireland, which is also a founder of the ERM, is not examined because of lack of monthly data for some of the relevant variables. Luxembourg, which forms an Economic Union together with Belgium, is not examined either.

[29] The sample period for France is shorter due to some missing observations (in monthly frequency) after October 1987 for the chosen money stock. See data appendix.

[30] The data is from the International Financial Statistics of the International Monetary Fund. I thank Boo Sjöö for providing me with his programs to transform the data series into free format data sets. Those programs are described in Sjöö (1987).

we make a slight change in the definition of dc_j and fr_j. These two variables have been previously defined, respectively, as changes in the domestic component and foreign component of the monetary base relative to the monetary base in the beginning of each period. In our empirical application, the changes in the two components of the monetary base are weighted by the monetary base in the beginning of the data sample. We adopt this procedure in order to make possible the interpretation of the cumulative impulse responses of the two variables. The cumulative impulse responses of dc_j and fr_j should, then, be interpreted as the cumulated changes in the domestic and foreign components of the monetary base relative to the monetary base in the beginning of the first period. Note further that this way of defining dc_j and fr_j allows us to add the cumulative impulse responses of the two variables in order to obtain the cumulative change in the monetary base relative to its level at the beginning of the first period.

The variable fr deserves a further note. One of the problems when studying intervention in foreign exchange markets is the lack of public official statistics. This is usually solved through the use of changes in international reserves as a proxy for intervention. Moreover, since it is impossible to disaggregate the amount of intervention by the different exchange markets, a strategy commonly used in empirical work is to attribute the change in foreign reserves solely to one market. These procedures seem particularly appropriate in the case of the non-Germany ERM members and are also adopted in this work. We use the change in the stock of foreign reserves as a proxy for intervention in the DM exchange market. This procedure is based on the following grounds:

(i) As noted in section 3.2, it seems that ERM countries have tacitly agreed that the Bundesbank should intervene in the U.S. dollar exchange market while the remaining members take the responsibility of keeping the intra-ERM exchange rates within EMS bands. Although non-Germany ERM countries have also made use of U.S. dollars, most of these operations were EMS related. The need to sometimes resort to third currencies was the result of the constraints imposed by the design of the ERM which requires permission for allowing intra-marginal interventions to be carried out with members' currencies.

(ii) Given the central role of the DM in the EMS, a country can defend the grid of ERM cross parities by simply intervening in the exchange market of the German currency. Intervention in the DM exchange market by a given country has indirect implications on the exchange rates of this country's currency against the remaining ERM currencies.

(iii) The difference between the changes in the official reserve holdings and the amount of intervention can be explained by the use of the credit lines under the rules of the VSTF mechanism of the ERM. However, since these credit lines are only used for marginal intervention and marginal intervention has little weight in overall intervention (see Table 2.2), the use of the VSTF is not very significant.[31] Furthermore, since our study

[31] The Commission of the European Communities (1983) reports that (page 119) "... *severe pressures in the foreign exchange market were countered by substantial*

focuses on interventions that try to counter a *trend* in the exchange rate rather than *daily* smoothing operations, the use by a given country of short-term credit lines - as in the case of the VSTF - is not matched by its partner in the near future and is, therefore, sooner or later reflected in the stock of international reserves. These time lags between intervention and changes in reserves are captured by the lag structure of the VARs.

The set of variables used in the models is, thus, the following:[32]

s_j = first difference of the log of exchange rate of country j's currency against the Deutsche mark

fr_j = change in international reserves in country j (evaluated at the period's average exchange rate) divided by the monetary base at the beginning of the first period of the data sample

dc_j = change in country j's domestic component of monetary base divided by the monetary base at the beginning of the first period of the data sample

$(y_j - y_{Ger})$ = first difference of the gap between the log of country j's real income and the log of German real income (real incomes are proxied by industrial production indeces)

$(i_j - i_{Ger})'$ = first difference of the differential between short-term nominal interest rates in country j and in Germany

m_{Ger} = first difference of the log of the German money stock[33]

In referring to specific countries, the index j will be substituted by Bel, Den, Fr, It, and Hol for Belgium, Denmark, France, Italy, and the Netherlands, respectively.

Plots of the time series and augmented Dickey-Fuller tests[34] (not reported) show that all the variables above are stationary. This is not surprising given that they are defined in first difference form.[35]

The first five variables in the list above are the endogenous variables in the model, while m_{Ger} is taken as exogenous. We also allow for an intercept in each of the equations in the five VAR models. Other exogenous variables to be added to each of the equations in the model are realignment related dummy variables. Although the EMS has undergone various realignments during the period under

intervention (by Italian authorities) - *the official reserves fell by LIT 4.500.000 million in two months ...*". This quotation is a clear illustration that most of exchange market intervention is reflected in the stock of official reserves.

[32]See Appendix 3.A for a detailed description of the variables.

[33]We use M1 as the German money stock. This is the stance also adopted by Gros (1989).

[34]See Dickey and Fuller (1981).

[35]The only variable which can be stationary in levels during the period under investigation is the income growth differential between the Netherlands and Germany.

investigation, many of the realignments did not lead to a clear break in the exchange rate series. What actually happened was that the market exchange rates, which were in the upper limit of the band, were ratified by the new bands which moved upwards. Dummy variables are used only for those realignment months in which clear breaks in the data series were observed.[36]

Two alternative ways have been adopted in the literature to estimate VAR models. While some researchers use variables in levels, others prefer variables in differences in order to achieve stationarity. In the latter case, however, Engle and Granger (1987) argue that an error-correcting explanatory variable should be added to the model when the set of variables in the VAR are cointegrated. Since our variables are in first differences - following the exchange market equilibrium model presented in section 3.2 - we have adopted the two-step strategy of Hall (1986) to obtain the error-correcting terms. The VARs for each country were estimated both with and without explanatory correction terms but the results from the two versions were similar. The results reported are for the model without error-correcting terms.

3.5. Results

The results reported below are based on VAR models whose exact number of lags is presented in Appendix 3.B. In order to arrive at the final structure, we used a three-step procedure. Since the lag length of a VAR model has to be truncated at some order, we first imposed a maximum of eight lags on each variable in every equation. At the second stage, likelihood ratio tests of the hypothesis that each variable entered each equation with four lags was performed against the alternative of eight lags. The null hypothesis was not rejected for any of the five countries. In the third and last stage, the model was subject to further adjustments in the number of lags in order to ensure non-autocorrelated residuals. Autocorrelation in the residuals was checked using the m-test proposed by Breusch (1978) and Godfrey (1978).

The VARs were estimated using ordinary least squares, while for the contemporaneous models we used the method of moments, as in Bernanke (1986). The resulting variance/covariance and correlation matrices of the residuals, as well as the matrices of the contemporaneous coefficients, are provided in Appendix 3.B.

For our purposes, two correlation coefficients of the residuals are of particular interest. Focusing on the correlations between the innovations of the exchange rate variable and the foreign exchange intervention variable, the negative figures for Denmark (-0.15), France (-0.15), Italy (-0.19), and the Netherlands (-0.16) are the first indicators that these countries "leaned against the wind" right at the moment that shocks in the market exchange rate occurred. Such behavior does not seem to apply to Belgium given the positive, although small, value (0.03) of the correlation coefficient between the innovations in s_{Bel} and fr_{Bel}.

[36] The dummies relate to the following countries and months: February 1982 for Belgium; November 1979 for Denmark; October 1981, June 1982, March 1983, and April 1986 for France; March 1981, October 1981, and July 1985 for Italy.

Focusing on the correlations between the innovations of the foreign and domestic components of the monetary base, one finds that they are negative as expected, and large in magnitude. The figures are -0.95, -0.91, -0.83, -0.60, and -0.58 for the Netherlands, Belgium, Denmark, France and Italy, respectively. These correlation coefficients could either be the result of contemporaneous sterilization or contemporaneous offsetting. Given our discussion in section 3.3, we can assume that these high and negative correlations are the first signs that interventions have been immediately sterilized.

The indications from the coefficients of correlation are confirmed by the signs of the estimated coefficients of the contemporaneous models, the λs in the system of equations (3.12). The "leaning-against-the-wind" reaction by central banks in the period that shocks in the exchange rate occurred is depicted by the element b_{23} in the matrices of the contemporaneous models presented in Appendix 3.B. The computed figures, with the expected signs, are -5.89, -0.96, -0.71 and -1.39 for Denmark, France, Italy and the Netherlands, respectively. The coefficient for Belgium shows a positive sign of 0.23, meaning that the Belgian monetary authorities "bent with the wind" (although on a small scale) whenever a shock in the exchange rate occurred. Note, however, that these five countries fully sterilized the foreign exchange operations carried out during the period. The contemporaneous coefficients of sterilization range from -1.10 for Belgium, to -0.99 for France.

Among the countries that contemporaneously "leaned against the wind", Denmark is an extreme case with a very high absolute value for the coefficient. A one percent positive shock (i.e., depreciation) in the DKR/DM exchange rate leads the Danish stock of international reserves to decrease immediately and at a very high rate, at least in comparison with the other countries. The domestic currency counterpart of the immediate decrease of foreign reserves represents almost 6 percent of the whole stock of the monetary base. This is an indication that the one-sided intervention in the DKR/DM exchange market had, during the period under investigation, highly destabilizing effects on the stock of international reserves held by the Danish central bank.

When a variable in the system is shocked, all endogenous variables adjust dynamically to a new long-run equilibrium. In order to analyze how ERM central banks reacted - both in the foreign exchange market as well as the money market - when an exchange rate depreciation occurred, we have assessed the effects of a one-shot depreciation of one percent. The corresponding cumulative impulse response functions of dc, fr, mb, and s, for a horizon of 30 months, are plotted in Figures 3.1-3.5. In order to make comparisons across countries easier, selected values of the response functions for 1, 4, 9, 19, and 29 months after the shock are provided in Table 3.1.

The impulse response functions show that "leaning against the wind" in the DM exchange market is a feature common to the five ERM central banks. In fact, the initial exchange rate depreciation is reflected in a permanent fall in the stock of international reserves. This also applies to Belgium which, as we have seen, shows a contemporaneous behavior that points in the opposite direction. "Leaning against the wind" is, thus, performed with some time lag in the Belgian franc/Deutsche mark foreign exchange market. This result highlights the appropriateness of the use of a dynamic model for studying interventions.

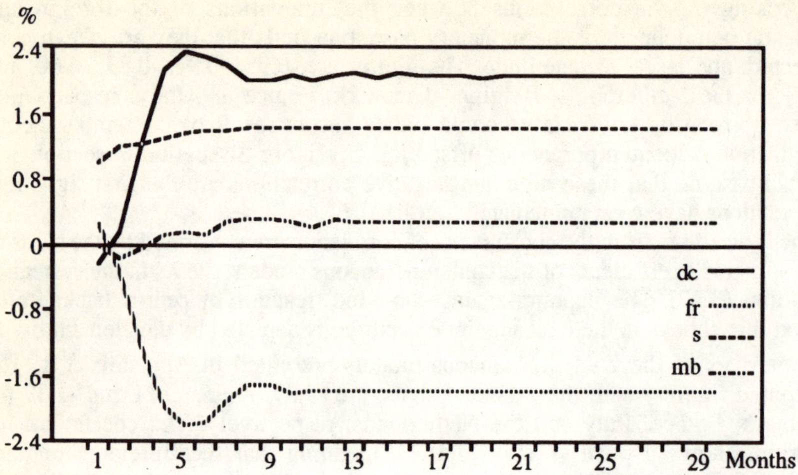

Fig. 3.1 - Cumulative responses to a 1% depreciation, Belgium

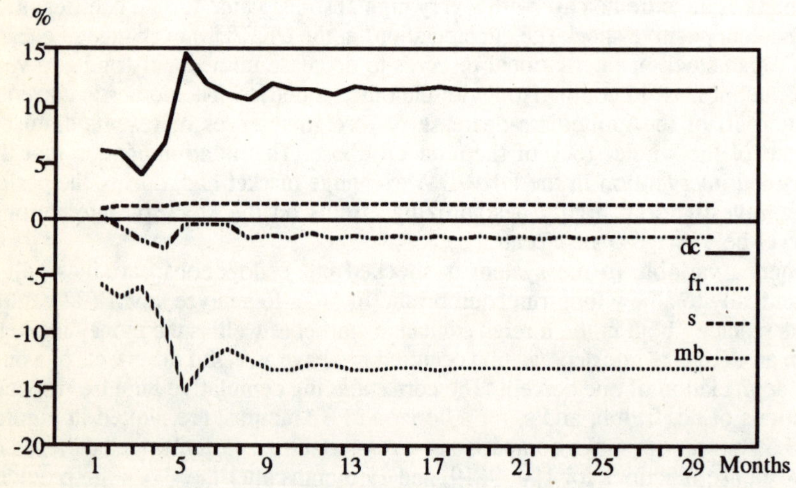

Fig. 3.2 - Cumulative responses to a 1% depreciation, Denmark

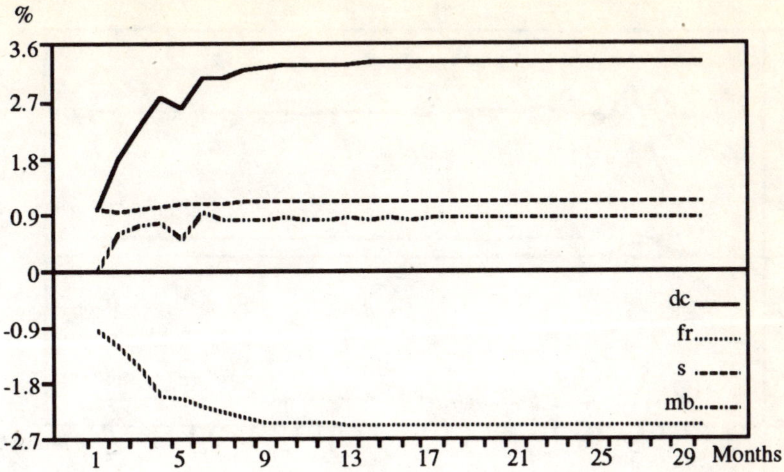

Fig. 3.3 - Cumulative responses to a 1% depreciation, France

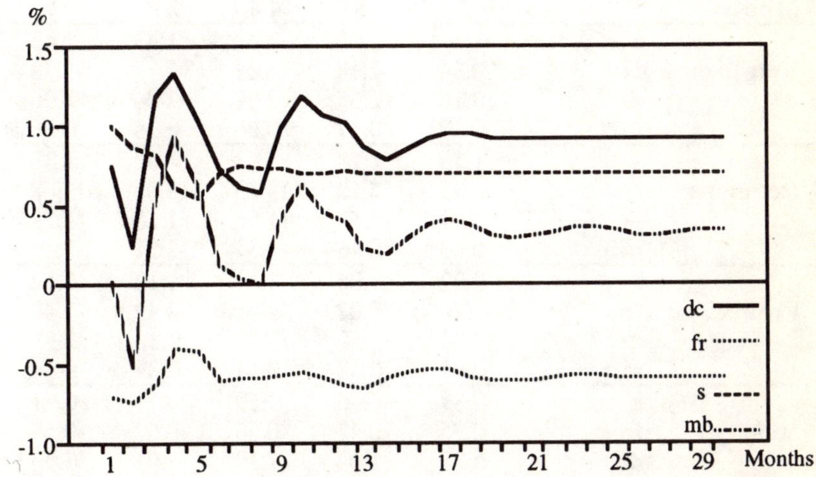

Fig. 3.4 - Cumulative responses to a 1% depreciation, Italy

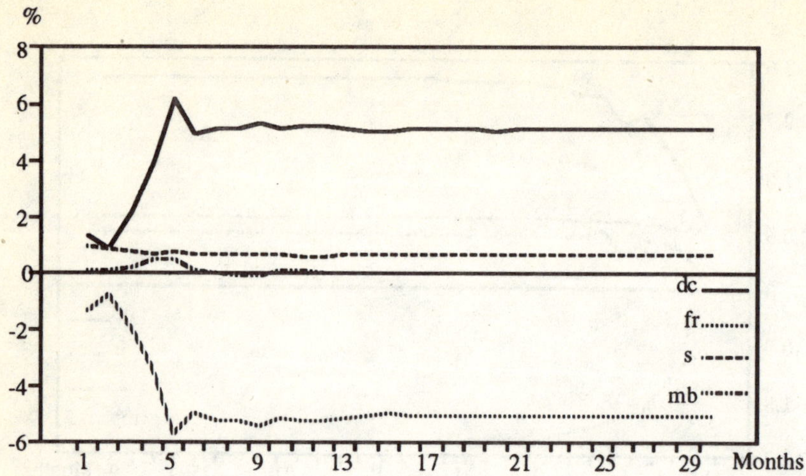

Fig. 3.5 - Cumulative responses to a 1% depreciation, the Netherlands

Table 3.1 - Cumulative responses to a 1% depreciation

Month		2	5	10	20	30
	s	1.18	1.35	1.42	1.43	1.43
Belgium	fr	-0.34	-2.18	-1.81	-1.78	-1.78
	dc	0.16	2.35	2.07	2.06	2.06
	mb	-0.18	0.17	0.26	0.28	0.28
	s	1.10	1.28	1.33	1.32	1.32
Denmark	fr	-6.95	-15.10	-13.13	-13.06	-13.08
	dc	6.07	14.64	11.56	11.55	11.59
	mb	-0.88	-0.46	-1.57	-1.51	-1.49
	s	0.92	1.06	1.11	1.12	1.12
France	fr	-1.20	-2.07	-2.45	-2.49	-2.49
	dc	1.81	2.59	3.29	3.33	3.33
	mb	0.61	0.52	0.84	0.84	0.84
	s	0.87	0.56	0.69	0.71	0.71
Italy	fr	-0.75	-0.42	-0.56	-0.62	-0.59
	dc	0.23	1.04	1.19	0.91	0.93
	mb	-0.52	0.62	0.63	0.29	0.34
	s	0.81	0.74	0.64	0.64	0.64
Netherl.	fr	-0.81	-5.70	-5.12	-5.05	-5.06
	dc	0.82	6.15	5.14	5.03	5.06
	mb	0.01	0.45	0.02	-0.02	0.00

A remarkable result shown by the impulse response functions is the huge loss of foreign reserves in Denmark following the initial 1 percent exchange rate depreciation. The ultimate loss of foreign reserves, evaluated in domestic currency, represents 13.08 percent of the initial monetary base. The long-run equilibrium following the 1 percent depreciation also leads to a relatively high loss of international reserves in the Netherlands, 5.06 percent of the initial monetary base.

Apart from Italy, the remaining countries also end up with losses of foreign reserves that are larger than that observed in the month of the initial depreciation. The total loss of foreign reserves, evaluated in domestic currency, represents 1.78 percent of the initial Belgian monetary base and 2.49 percent of the initial French monetary base. The Italian central bank is alone in recovering some of the foreign reserves used for interventions in the very month in which the depreciation occurs. The loss of foreign reserves ensuing the depreciation represents 0.71 percent of the initial monetary base and the recovery is of the order of 0.12 percentage points.

Another aspect revealed by the impulse response functions is that, parallel to "leaning against the wind", all ERM central banks systematically sterilize their exchange market operations. The Danish monetary authorities sterilize 88.6 percent of the ultimate change in international reserves, while the long-run equilibrium in Belgium and France leads to increases in their respective monetary bases. The fact that Denmark is the only country that does not fully sterilize can either be due to a strategy that aims at influencing the market exchange rate or the result of the authorities' inability to sterilize the observed huge "leaning-against-the-wind" impacts.

Concerning the long-run effects on the exchange rates, Italy and the Netherlands are the only countries that are able to smooth out the initial depreciation. Out of the initial 1 percent increase in the exchange rate, the lasting depreciations are of the order of 0.71 percent and 0.64 percent for the Italian lira and the Dutch guilder, respectively. In contrast, Belgium, Denmark and France are not able to counter the initial change in the exchange rate. Belgium ends up with a depreciation of 1.43 percent, Denmark with 1.32 percent, and the French franc's total depreciation amounts to 1.12 percent.

Similar to the coefficients of the contemporaneous models, the lasting effects on the exchange rates and on foreign reserves show that the intensity of intervention varied a lot from country to country. This intensity might even have been higher in some countries if capital controls had not been used. Figures for the ratio fr_j/s_j, showing the time evolution of the "leaning against the wind", are presented in Table 3.2 for selected months.

Table 3.2 - "Leaning against the wind": (fr_j/s_j) evolution

Months	Belgium	Denmark	France	Italy	Netherl.
2	0.29	6.31	1.30	0.87	1.00
5	1.62	11.84	1.96	0.75	7.65
10	1.28	9.89	2.21	0.81	8.02
20	1.25	9.86	2.23	0.87	7.83
30	1.25	9.87	2.23	0.83	7.86

Note: The negative signs of the ratios are omitted.

The Table shows that the initial 1 percent depreciation implied a very high long-run "leaning-against-the-wind" coefficient for both Denmark and the Netherlands. Despite the fact that the total loss of foreign reserves in Denmark was more than twice as important as that of the Netherlands, as shown in Table 3.1, the ratio fr_j/s_j for the two countries are not very different from each other. This is the result of the partial success of the Dutch monetary authorities, relative to the Danish, in countering the initial depreciation of their currency.

Concerning the two countries that succeded in reversing the path of the market exchange rate, the costs of countering the initial depreciation are much higher in the Netherlands than in Italy. While the Italian monetary authorities counter 0.29 percent of the initial depreciation with a relative loss of reserves of 0.59 percent, the Dutch central bank loses 5.06 percent of its foreign reserves to recover 0.36 percent of the initial depreciation. If a country fails to counter the initial depreciation and keeps losing foreign reserves, the cost of intervention is infinite. This has, actually, been the case in the remaining three countries. They keep on losing foreign reserves without reversing any of the initial exchange rate depreciation.

3.6. Summary and conclusions

In this chapter we have characterized the foreign exchange market interventions of ERM central banks during the first eight years of the EMS, a period in which eleven realignments occurred. We have addressed the following three questions: How did ERM central banks react to changes in market exchange rates? i.e., did they "lean against the wind"? Did they sterilize exchange market intervention? Finally, was intervention by ERM central banks able to counter exchange rate trends? These questions were approached with the help of VAR estimations of a set of variables from the DM exchange market pressure model.

Our results show that the conflict between external and internal objectives is quite obvious. In order to maintain control over the money stock, monetary authorities in ERM countries sterilized the operations carried out in the exchange market. By adopting such behavior, they either did not succeed at all or only partially in countering market exchange rate movements. At the same time, they lost international reserves.

Furthermore, concerning this loss of international reserves, the predictions of Herring and Marston (1977) about the trade-off between the control of the monetary base and that of international reserves are confirmed by the results for Belgium, Denmark, France, and the Netherlands. The high degree of sterilization in the four countries enabled them to control the money stock. This, in turn, increased the magnitude of the offsetting capital flows. The adoption of the leaning-against-the-wind-cum-sterilization had dramatic consequences for the stability of the stock of foreign reserves of the Danish central bank and, to a lesser extent, the Dutch central bank.

Only in two countries, Italy and the Netherlands, were sterilized interventions able to partly counter the exchange rate trends.[37] However, to counter the depreciations, the costs of intervention were much higher in the Netherlands.

Our results imply that the adopted policies of intervention and sterilization led to opportunities to make profits in some of the ERM exchange markets. Besides the periods preceding the realignments, which often involve the entrance of speculators into the market, the impulse response functions show that, in the normal running of the EMS, the occurrence of a shock in the DM exchange rates of the Belgian franc, Danish krone, and French franc was a good signal to join the market. In fact, if speculators decided to join the market within six or seven months after the initial depreciation they would then make profits given that exchange rates depreciated further in the following months.

The poor results achieved by official foreign exchange intervention in the DM exchange markets are not surprising. If intervention was an effective instrument for keeping exchange rates within the bands, there wouldn't be need for realignments. What is surprising is that, despite these results, EMS countries insisted in intervening and sterilizing. The only plausible explanation for this lies in the design of the ERM. While the ERM explicitly requires its members to intervene, it does not specify that the money stock of member countries should converge to the German levels and, thus, does not prohibit the sterilization of intervention operations in the DM exchange market. This implies that EMS countries have likely exchanged the (lack of) stability in the stock of international reserves for monetary autonomy relative to the pattern followed by Germany. This is an issue to be investigated with more detail in chapter 5.

On the whole, the main lesson from the results of this chapter is that the design of an exchange regime with fixed rates should set monetary rules in an explicit way rather than simply rely on rules of intervention.

The conclusions from this chapter leave us with a puzzle. On the one hand, ERM countries were unable to successfully counter exchange rate trends. On the other hand, the Dutch monetary authorities have been able to keep the guilder exchange rates within the same DM band since the March 1983 realignment. Can it be that the Dutch or all the ERM central banks had an alternative to intervention for achieving their exchange rate targets? This question is examined in the next chapter. We have further observed that the ERM countries generally adopted a policy of sterilization. The assessment of sterilization is often used in order to check whether a country follows an autonomous monetary policy. According to our results, it would appear that all ERM countries followed monetary policies that were independent from the developments in DM exchange markets. This being the case, how then was it possible for the guilder/DM rate to remain fixed for so many years? This question is discussed in chapter 5.

[37] Our results are, thus, mixed concerning the effectiveness of sterilized intervention, often discussed in the literature and mentioned in the introduction to this chapter. Some effectiveness is observed for Italy and the Netherlands, but the results point in the opposite direction for the remaining three countries.

Appendix 3.A - Variable definitions and data sources

Monthly data is taken from the International Financial Statistics of the International Monetary Fund. In the following list, a prime denotes the first difference of the variables in levels.

s_j : first difference of the log of spot exchange rate, defined as the number of domestic currency units per DM. It is the result of triangular arbitrage based on the U.S. dollar exchange rates (*line we* for Belgium and *line ae* for the remaining countries).

y_{Ger} : first difference of the log of German real income, seasonally adjusted. It is proxied by the industrial production index, seasonally adjusted (*line 66..c*).

y_j : first difference of the log of real income, seasonally adjusted. It is proxied by the industrial production index, seasonally adjusted (*line 66..b* for Belgium and *line 66..c* for the remaining countries).

m_{Ger} : first difference of the log of the German money supply, seasonally adjusted (*line 34..b*).

i_{Ger} : German nominal interest rate (*line 60bs*).

i_j : Nominal interest rate (*line 60c* for Belgium, *line 60bs* for France, and *line 60b* for Denmark, Italy, and the Netherlands).

$(i_j - i_{Ger})'$: first difference of the differential between i_j and i_{Ger}.

MS_j : Money stock, narrow definition of money (M1), end-of-period data (*line 34*).

FR_j : Stock of foreign reserves in U.S. dollars, end-of-period data (line *1l.d*).

SA_j : Period average exchange rate, defined as the number of domestic currency units per U.S. dollar (*line wf* for Belgium and *line rf* for the remaining countries).

MB_j : Monetary base, end-of-period data (*line 14*).

fr_j^* : Domestic currency counterpart of the monthly change in foreign reserves (FR_j), relative to the monetary base (MB_j) in the beginning of the month. Since FR_j are measured in U.S. dollars, we evaluate the change using the period average exchange rate (SA_j).

DC_j : Domestic component of the monetary base.

dc_j^* : Monthly change in DC_j relative to the monetary base (MB_j) in the beginning of the month.
To get DC_j and dc_j^* we follow the procedure described in Blejer (1977). The monetary base (MB_j) can be decomposed into two parts, the domestic and the foreign components

$$MB_j = DC_j + FC_j \tag{A.1}$$

where FC_j denotes the foreign part and is made up of successive cumulations of $[FR_j'.SA_j]$ in order for capital gains and losses on foreign exchange not to be reflected in MB_j.
In rates of change, the above expression becomes

$$\frac{MB_j'}{MB_j} = \lambda \frac{DC_j'}{DC_j} + (1 - \lambda) \frac{FR_j'.SA_j}{FC_j} \tag{A.2}$$

where $\lambda = \frac{DC_j}{MB_j}$.

The definition of money supply is given by

$$MS_j = a_j \, . \, MB_j \tag{A.3}$$

where a_j is the money multiplier. Combining (A.3), properly transformed, with (A.2), we obtain

$$dc_j^* = \frac{MS_j'}{MS_j} - fr_j^* - \frac{a_j'}{a_j} \tag{A.4}$$

For all sample countries, the three terms of the right-hand side of (A.4) can be computed except for Belgium since MS_j is not available on a monthly basis. For Belgium we obtain DC_j in the following way: first we compute $DC_j' = [MB_j' - FR_j'.SA_j]$ and then we cumulate these changes with an initial stock given by ($MB_j - FR_j.SA_j$), using the figures from January 1969.

$mb_{j,t}$: Index for the monetary base defined as

$$mb_{j,t} = mb_{j,t-1} \left[\left(dc_{j,t}^* + fr_{j,t}^* \right) + 1 \right] , \quad \text{where } mb_{j,0} = 1.$$

dc_j : Change in the domestic component of the monetary base, defined in terms of the monetary base index:

$$dc_{j,t} = dc^*_{j,t} \cdot mb_{j,t-1}$$

It can be interpreted as the change in the domestic component relative to the monetary base in period zero.

fr_j : Change in the foreign component of the monetary base, defined in terms of the monetary base index:

$$fr_{j,t} = fr^*_{j,t} \cdot mb_{j,t-1}$$

It can be interpreted as the change in the foreign component relative to the monetary base in period zero.

Appendix 3.B.1 - Other VAR results for Belgium

Specification of the VAR model and autocorrelation tests

	dc_{Bel}	fr_{Bel}	s_{Bel}	$(i_{Bel}-i_{Ger})'$	$y_{Bel}-y_{Ger}$	m_{Ger}	m(12)
dc_{Bel}	1-4	1-4	1-4	1-4	1-4	1-4	0.972
fr_{Bel}	1-4	1-4	1-4	1-4	1-4	1-4	0.796
s_{Bel}	1-4	1-4	1-4	1-4	1-4	1-4	0.202
$(i_{Bel}i_{Ger})'$	1-4	1-4	1-4	1-4	1-4	1-3	0.068
$y_{Bel}-y_{Ger}$	1-4	1-4	1-4	1-4	1-4	1-4	0.299

• The (i,j) entry gives the lags of variable j used in the estimation of variable i.
• The column m(12) contains the probabilities of no autocorrelation in the error terms. The allowed maximum order of autocorrelation was set at 12.

Variance/covariance matrix of the residuals

	dc	fr	s	int. rate	income
dc	0.202E-02				
fr	-0.152E-02	0.139E-02			
s	-0.101E-05	0.492E-05	0.257E-04		
int. rate	-0.414E-04	0.834E-05	-0.187E-05	0.222E-04	
income	0.383E-04	-0.618E-04	0.810E-06	0.188E-04	0.482E-03

Correlation matrix of the residuals

	dc	fr	s	int. rate	income
dc					
fr	-0.9076				
s	-0.0044	0.0260			
int. rate	-0.1949	0.0473	-0.0782		
income	0.0388	-0.0753	0.0073	0.1823	

Matrix of the contemporaneous coefficients

	dc	fr	s	int.rate	income
dc	1.000	1.097	0.000	0.000	0.061
fr	0.000	1.000	-0.227	0.000	0.000
s	0.000	0.000	1.000	0.105	0.000
int. rate	0.088	0.000	0.000	1.000	0.000
income	0.000	0.000	0.000	0.000	1.000

Variances of the "orthogonal" innovations

dc	fr	s	int. rate	income
0.356E-03	0.140E-02	0.256E-04	0.306E-04	0.482E-03

Appendix 3.B.2 - Other VAR results for Denmark

Specification of the VAR model and autocorrelation tests

	dc_{Den}	fr_{Den}	s_{Den}	$(i_{Den}-i_{Ger})'$	$y_{Den}-y_{Ger}$	m_{Ger}	m(12)
dc_{Den}	1-4	1-4	1-4	1-4	1-3	1-3	0.139
fr_{Den}	1-4	1-4	1-4	1-4	1-3	1-4	0.333
s_{Den}	1-4	1-4	1-4	1-4	1-4	1-4	0.718
$(i_{Den}-i_{Ger})'$	1-4	1-4	1-4	1-4	1-4	1-4	0.391
$y_{Den}-y_{Ger}$	1-4	1-4	1-4	1-4	1-4	1-4	0.144

• The (i,j) entry gives the lags of variable j used in the estimation of variable i.
• The column m(12) contains the probabilities of no autocorrelation in the error terms. The allowed maximum order of autocorrelation was set at 12.

Variance/covariance matrix of the residuals

	dc	fr	s	int. rate	income
dc	0.850E-01				
fr	-0.574E-01	0.560E-01			
s	0.117E-03	-0.214E-03	0.368E-04		
int. rate	0.387E-04	0.631E-04	-0.210E-04	0.447E-03	
income	0.790E-03	0.777E-04	-0.160E-04	-0.865E-04	0.704E-03

Correlation matrix of the residuals

	dc	fr	s	int. rate	income
dc					
fr	-0.8325				
s	0.0662	-0.1490			
int. rate	0.0063	0.0126	-0.1636		
income	0.1021	0.0124	-0.0994	-0.1542	

Matrix of the contemporaneous coefficients

	dc	fr	s	int. rate	income
dc	1.000	1.036	0.000	0.000	-1.235
fr	0.000	1.000	5.894	0.000	0.000
s	0.000	0.000	1.000	0.049	0.000
int. rate	-0.009	0.000	0.000	1.000	0.000
income	0.000	0.000	0.000	0.000	1.000

Variances of the "orthogonal" innovations

dc	fr	s	int. rate	income
0.250E-01	0.547E-01	0.358E-04	0.453E-03	0.704E-03

Appendix 3.B.3 - Other VAR results for France

Specification of the VAR model and autocorrelation tests

	dc_{Fr}	fr_{Fr}	s_{Fr}	$(i_{Fr}-i_{Ger})'$	$y_{Fr}-y_{Ger}$	m_{Ger}	m(12)
dc_{Fr}	1-4	1-4	1-4	1-4	1-4	1-4	0.740
fr_{Fr}	1-4	1-4	1-4	1-4	1-4	1-4	0.308
s_{Fr}	1-4	1-4	1-4	1-4	1-4	1-4	0.203
$(i_{Fr}-i_{Ger})'$	1-4	1-4	1-4	1-4	1-4	1-4	0.176
$y_{Fr}-y_{Ger}$	1-4	1-4	1-4	1-4	1-4	1-4	0.975

• The (i,j) entry gives the lags of variable j used in the estimation of variable i.
• The column m(12) contains the probabilities of no autocorrelation in the error terms. The allowed maximum order of autocorrelation was set at 12.

Variance/covariance matrix of the residuals

	dc	fr	s	int. rate	income
dc	0.650E-02				
fr	-0.229E-02	0.220E-02			
s	0.181E-03	-0.517E-04	0.508E-04		
int. rate	0.973E-04	-0.835E-04	0.161E-05	0.333E-04	
income	0.260E-04	0.518E-04	-0.347E-05	0.173E-04	0.321E-03

Correlation matrix of the residuals

	dc	fr	s	int. rate	income
dc					
fr	-0.6044				
s	0.3148	-0.1546			
int. rate	0.2090	-0.3083	0.0390		
income	0.0180	0.0617	-0.0271	0.1675	

Matrix of the contemporaneous coefficients

	dc	fr	s	int. rate	income
dc	1.000	0.987	0.000	0.000	-0.240
fr	0.000	1.000	0.961	0.000	0.000
s	0.000	0.000	1.000	-0.035	0.000
int. rate	-0.003	0.000	0.000	1.000	0.000
income	0.000	0.000	0.000	0.000	1.000

Variances of the "orthogonal" innovations

dc	fr	s	int. rate	income
0.411E-02	0.215E-02	0.508E-04	0.329E-04	0.321E-03

Appendix 3.B.4 - Other VAR results for Italy

Specification of the VAR model and autocorrelation tests

	dc_{It}	fr_{It}	s_{It}	$(i_{It}-i_{Ger})'$	$y_{It}-y_{Ger}$	m_{Ger}	m(12)
dc_{It}	1-5	1-5	1-4	1-4	1-4	1-5	0.143
fr_{It}	1-4	1-4	1-4	1-4	1-4	1-4	0.200
s_{It}	1-4	1-4	1-4	1-4	1-4	1-4	0.136
$(i_{It}-i_{Ger})'$	1-4	1-4	1-4	1-4	1-4	1-4	0.318
$y_{It}-y_{Ger}$	1-4	1-4	1-4	1-4	1-4	1-4	0.492

• The (i,j) entry gives the lags of variable j used in the estimation of variable i.
• The column m(12) contains the probabilities of no autocorrelation in the error terms. The allowed maximum order of autocorrelation was set at 12.

Variance/covariance matrix of the residuals

	dc	fr	s	int. rate	income
dc	0.256E-02				
fr	-0.847E-03	0.823E-03			
s	0.214E-04	-0.395E-04	0.516E-04		
int. rate	-0.330E-04	0.220E-04	-0.429E-05	0.310E-04	
income	0.137E-03	-0.231E-04	-0.143E-04	-0.324E-04	0.615E-03

Correlation matrix of the residuals

	dc	fr	s	int. rate	income
dc					
fr	-0.5829				
s	0.0590	-0.1916			
int. rate	-0.1170	0.1379	-0.1073		
income	0.1094	-0.0325	-0.0803	-0.2349	

Matrix of the contemporaneous coefficients

	dc	fr	s	int. rate	income
dc	1.000	1.038	0.000	0.000	-0.184
fr	0.000	1.000	0.715	0.000	0.000
s	0.000	0.000	1.000	0.137	0.000
int. rate	0.002	0.000	0.000	1.000	0.000
income	0.000	0.000	0.000	0.000	1.000

Variances of the "orthogonal" innovations

dc	fr	s	int. rate	income
0.167E-02	0.793E-03	0.510E-04	0.309E-04	0.615E-03

Appendix 3.B.5 - Other VAR results for the Netherlands

Specification of the VAR model and autocorrelation tests

	dc_{Hol}	fr_{Hol}	s_{Hol}	$(i_{Hol}-i_{Ger})'$	$y_{Hol}-y_{Ger}$	m_{Ger}	m(12)
dc_{Hol}	1-4	1-4	1-4	1-4	1-4	1-4	0.863
fr_{Hol}	1-4	1-4	1-4	1-4	1-4	1-4	0.444
s_{Hol}	1-4	1-4	1-4	1-4	1-4	1-4	0.231
$(i_{Hol}-i_{Ger})'$	1-4	1-4	1-4	1-4	1-4	1-4	0.057
$y_{Hol}-y_{Ger}$	1-4	1-4	1-4	1-4	1-4	1-4	0.413

• The (i,j) entry gives the lags of variable j used in the estimation of variable i.
• The column m(12) contains the probabilities of no autocorrelation in the error terms. The allowed maximum order of autocorrelation was set at 12.

Variance/covariance matrix of the residuals

	dc	fr	s	int. rate	income
dc	0.296E-02				
fr	-0.262E-02	0.254E-02			
s	0.415E-04	-0.408E-04	0.242E-04		
int. rate	-0.286E-04	0.432E-04	-0.131E-04	0.526E-04	
income	-0.767E-04	0.560E-04	0.141E-04	-0.401E-04	0.728E-03

Correlation matrix of the residuals

	dc	fr	s	int. rate	income
dc					
fr	-0.9537				
s	0.1549	-0.1647			
int. rate	-0.0725	0.1182	-0.3673		
income	-0.0522	0.0412	0.1061	-0.2051	

Matrix of the contemporaneous coefficients

	dc	fr	s	int. rate	income
dc	1.000	1.030	0.000	0.000	0.026
fr	0.000	1.000	1.394	0.000	0.000
s	0.000	0.000	1.000	0.284	0.000
int. rate	-0.056	0.000	0.000	1.000	0.000
income	0.000	0.000	0.000	0.000	1.000

Variances of the "orthogonal" innovations

dc	fr	s	int. rate	income
0.267E-03	0.247E-02	0.210E-04	0.649E-04	0.728E-03

Appendix B.2 - Other VAR results for the Netherlands

[illegible]

[illegible]	[illegible]	[illegible]	[illegible]	[illegible]	[illegible]	[illegible]	[illegible]

[illegible]

Variance-covariance matrix of the residuals

				int. rate	income
e	[illegible]				
p	[illegible]	[illegible]			
s	[illegible]	[illegible]	[illegible]		
int. rate	[illegible]	[illegible]	[illegible]	[illegible]	
income	[illegible]	[illegible]	[illegible]	[illegible]	[illegible]

Correlation matrix of the residuals

	e	p	s	int. rate	income
e					
p	[illegible]				
s	[illegible]	[illegible]			
int. rate	[illegible]	[illegible]	[illegible]		
income	[illegible]	[illegible]	[illegible]	[illegible]	

Matrix of the contemporaneous correlations

	e	p	s	int. rate	income
e	1.000	[illegible]	[illegible]	[illegible]	[illegible]
p	[illegible]	[illegible]	[illegible]	[illegible]	[illegible]
s	[illegible]	[illegible]	1.000	[illegible]	[illegible]
int. rate	[illegible]	[illegible]	0.000	[illegible]	0.000
income	[illegible]	[illegible]	[illegible]	[illegible]	[illegible]

Variances of the orthogonal innovations

e	p	s	int. rate	income
[illegible]	[illegible]	[illegible]	[illegible]	[illegible]

CHAPTER 4
"Leaning against the wind" through interest rate management: The EMS in the period from 1979 to 1988

4.1. Introduction

In the previous chapter, we have seen that during the period from 1979 to 1988, all ERM central banks intervened in the foreign exchange markets in a "leaning-against-the-wind" manner. The expected behavior in a cooperative exchange rate regime was, therefore, followed. However, a feature which is also common to the investigated foreign exchange markets is that interventions were sterilized by offsetting operations in the money markets. The combination of these two reactions - "leaning against the wind" and sterilization - made the exchange market intervention an ineffective instrument for countering the trends in the exchange rates. Furthermore, the use of sterilized interventions with the purpose of countering depreciations, has shown to be an extremely costly policy - at least in some countries - in terms of the loss of foreign reserves.

The purpose of this chapter is to analyze whether the management of market interest rates in ERM countries contributed to achieving exchange market targets both in terms of exchange rates and the recovery of foreign reserves.[38] The countries and periods covered are the same analyzed in chapter 3. In the previous chapter, we were primarily concerned with the inter-relationships between exchange rates, foreign reserves and the domestic component of the monetary base - the dashed arrows in Figure 4.1. In this chapter, we focus on the relationships between interest rates and market exchange rates, on the one hand, and interest rates and foreign reserves, on the other - the solid arrows in Figure 4.1.

---

[38]This behavior was formally modeled by Kostiainen and Taimio (1988) who developed a model where the interest rate "leans against the wind". The model is thought to explain the successful actions by Nordic central banks in the 1980s in defending exchange rates by temporarily raising short-term interest rates, at times to very high levels.

The management of interest rates can also be used to achieve other goals than foreign exchange market targets. For example, Joyce (1986) estimates the Canadian central bank interest rate as a reaction function to deviations from targets which are both internal (unemployment rate and inflation rate) and external (exchange rate and current account).

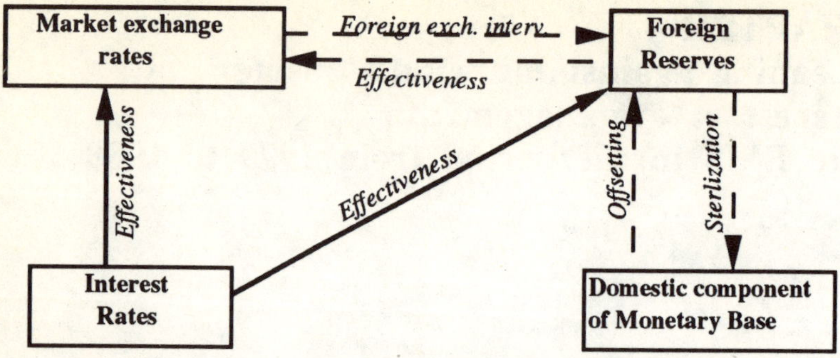

Figure 4.1 - "Leaning against the wind" through foreign exchange reserves and interest rates

The remaining part of the chapter is organized in four sections. Section 4.2 provides a brief and general discussion of the relationship between the interest rate and the foreign exchange market. Section 4.3 describes the methodology adopted for assessing whether ERM central banks, by managing market interest rates, were able to affect the Deutsche mark exchange rates and to recover international reserves. The data is also described in section 4.3 and the results and conclusions are presented in section 4.4.

4.2. Interest rate management and foreign exchange market effects

The manner in which an ERM central bank may affect the DM exchange market through changing the interest rate can be described with the help of expression (4.1) which reproduces the DM exchange market pressure model derived in the previous chapter.

$$s_j - fr_j = dc_j - m_{Ger} - \beta\,(y_j - y_{Ger}) + \alpha\,(i_j - i_{Ger})' \qquad (4.1)$$

where, as before,

s_j = rate of depreciation of currency j in terms of the DM;

fr_j = domestic currency counterpart of the change in foreign reserves in country j, weighted by the monetary base;

dc_j = change in the domestic credit component of country j, weighted by the monetary base;

m_{Ger} = percentage change in the German money stock;

$(y_j - y_{Ger})$ = income growth differential between country j and Germany;

$(i_j - i_{Ger})'$ = change in the interest rate differential between country j and Germany.

As discussed above, pressures on the intra-European DM exchange markets coming from changes in the variables on the right-hand side of (4.1) have been absorbed by changes in the exchange rate and changes in foreign reserves of the non-German ERM members. From expression (4.1), it follows that specific exchange rate and foreign reserve targets may be immediately achieved if $\alpha \neq 0$ and if the monetary authorities are able to affect, *ceteris paribus*, the domestic interest rates.

In defending the exchange rate bands, central banks may either increase or decrease domestic interest rates. Since the tendency in the EMS has been for the non-German currencies to depreciate against the DM, we shall focus our analysis on the efforts to defend the upper limits of the bands. When the DM exchange rate approaches the upper limit of the margins of fluctuation allowed by the ERM, the central bank in country j - the central bank responsible for defending the band - has only one option of interest rate management, namely to raise the interest rate.

The prediction of the direction of change in $(s_j\text{-}fr_j)$ resulting from an increase in the interest rate is not, however, unambiguous. The increase in $(i_j\text{-}i_{Ger})'$ leads to a decrease in the left-hand side of (4.1), if the band is credible or if the increase in the interest rate exceeds the realignment risk. When the band is credible nobody expects a realignment so that an increase in the domestic interest rate is equivalent to a better payoff for holding domestic assets. There is, thus, an increase in the demand for domestic currency and, therefore, an exchange rate appreciation and/or an increase in the stock of foreign reserves. The same applies when the band is not credible but the increase in the interest rate exceeds the probability of a realignment multiplied by the expected devaluation. However, if the band is not credible and the higher interest rate does not compensate the risk of a realignment, the interest rate change might be followed by an outflow of foreign reserves and/or a depreciation. In that case, the increase in $(i_j\text{-}i_{Ger})'$ would lead to an increase in the left-hand side of (4.1). This was the case in Sweden in the Fall of 1992, when short-term interest rates at the level of 500 percent were not successful in preventing an exchange rate crisis that eventually led to a devaluation and the abandonment of an exchange rate regime of shadowing the EMS. Similar situations of unsuccessful interest rate policies, aimed at affecting the foreign exchange markets, can be found in the EMS after the September 1992 crisis.

The two opposing effects of a change in the interest rate on the foreign exchange market discussed above can be identified with the sign of α in expression (4.1). An increase in the interest rate in a bid by the central bank to counteract devaluation pressures will have the desired effects only when α is negative. In this case, the central bank recovers foreign reserves and/or the domestic currency appreciates. If α is positive, similar attempts by the central bank would not be successful, leading only to an undesired loss of foreign reserves and/or a depreciation of the domestic currency.[39] Finally, an α approximately equal to zero means that the foreign exchange market does not respond to interest rate management.

[39] The predictions described here are somehow related to those of the flexible-price and sticky-price monetary approaches of exchange rate determination. What distinguishes these two approaches are just the hypothesized effects on the (floating) exchange rates resulting from changes in the interest rate. For a detailed description of the two approaches see, for example, Frankel (1979).

Besides these direct effects of interest rate management on the stock of foreign reserves and market exchange rates, indirect effects may also be relevant for the (non)achievement of the desired goals. Even when $\alpha<0$, interest rate surprises may not have the desired effects on the foreign exchange market if other variables simultaneously respond to interest rate shocks.

Since changes in the interest rate initiated by the central bank may, in theory, have different and even contradictory effects on the foreign exchange market, verification of the actual ability of the ERM central banks to counter a depreciation (appreciation) through the increase (decrease) of the domestic interest rate is a subject for empirical investigation.

4.3. Methodology and data

To assess whether ERM central banks have been able to obtain an appreciation of their currencies against the DM and/or to increase the stock of foreign reserves through unexpected increases in market interest rates, we use the VAR models already described in the previous chapter. These models assess the joint process followed by the variables s_j, fr_j, dc_j, (y_j-y_{Ger}), and $(i_j-i_{Ger})'$, defined in section 4.2. The ability of ERM central banks to counter a depreciation by resorting to increases in the domestic interest rate is assessed with the help of the exchange rate impulse response functions to a positive, one-shot shock in the interest rate differential. The same shock in the interest rate is used to compute the impulse response functions of the foreign reserves variable. These two functions trace the path to the new long-run equilibrium in the exchange market when the system is shocked by a change in the interest rate differential.[40]

Techniques for money market control to manage interest rates differ from country to country, depending on institutional market features. Instruments like the central bank discount rate, reserve ratios, open market operations, government lending or combinations of several of these can be used. Even an official speech or a simple announcement of future policies, if credible, might be enough to affect the market interest rate. Here we disregard the instruments actually adopted in each specific country and simply assume that monetary authorities can, in one way or another, affect short-term interest rates, if they wish to do so.

The interest rates used in the VARs are short-term rates (see the data appendix in chapter 3). They represent both the opportunity cost of not holding domestic currency and the cost at which those betting on a devaluation borrow domestic currency to acquire foreign currency. By affecting short-term interest rates, monetary authorities try to affect both the supply and the demand for domestic currency and, through it, the foreign exchange market.

---

[40]Our analysis does not require that all innovations in the domestic interest rate be the result of unexpected actions undertaken by the domestic central bank. The only requirement is that these actions are one of the possible sources of innovation.

4.4. Results and conclusions

The effects on the intra-European DM exchange rates resulting from a positive one-percent, one-shot shock in the interest rate differential between country j and Germany are plotted in Figure 4.2. This figure contains the cumulative impulse responses of the first differences of the DM exchange rates (s_j) for the Belgian franc, Danish krone, French franc, Italian lira, and Dutch guilder, for a horizon of 30 months.

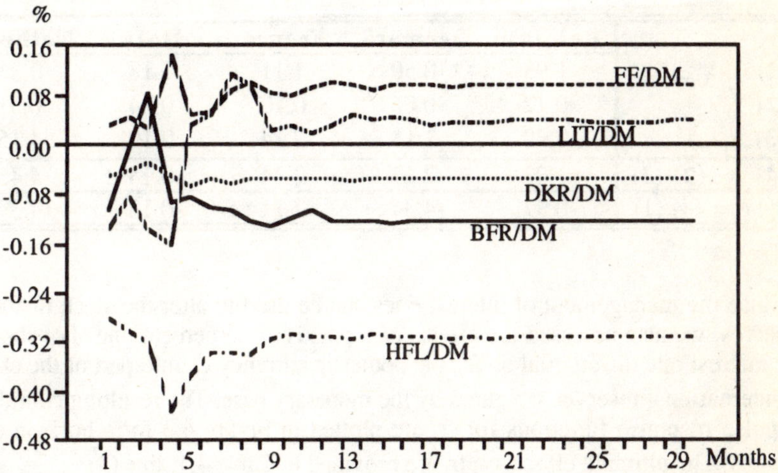

Figure 4.2 - Cumulative impulse responses of s_j to a 1% shock in $(i_j\text{-}i_{Ger})'$

The impulse response functions show that a positive shock in the differential between non-Germany ERM countries and Germany leads to an immediate appreciation of the BFR, DKR, and HFL against the DM. The effects on these three exchange rates are lasting, although temporarily reversed in the case of the Belgian franc. The HFL/DM exchange rate is the one showing the strongest appreciation.

In contrast, an interest rate shock leads to an immediate and permanent depreciation of the FF/DM exchange rate. A positive shock in the Italian/German interest rate differential in the period investigated leads to a temporary appreciation of the lira for the first quarter but the lasting effect is a depreciation of the Italian currency.

These results suggest that the Belgian, Danish and Dutch central banks could counter a depreciation by taking actions to increase the domestic interest rate. A more careful analysis shows, however, that only in the Netherlands the management of interest rates was ultimately successful. This can be seen from a comparison of the first two lines in Table 4.1 which contains the ultimate effects on interest rates and exchange rates resulting from a one-percent shock in the interest rate differential. To achieve a one-percent lasting appreciation of the BFR/DM exchange rate, Belgian monetary authorities would have to accept a permanent increase in interest rates amounting to 8.75 (i.e., 1.05/0.12) percentage points. A permanent increase of 8.33 percentage points would be required in Danish interest rates for the achievement of 1 percent appreciation of the DKR/DM exchange rate. The Netherlands is the only ERM member that, in practice, could use the management of interest rates to affect the exchange rate without excessively large interest rate movements.

Table 4.1 - Foreign exchange effects from a 1% shock in $(i_j - i_{Ger})'$

	Belgium	**Denmark**	**France**	**Italy**	**Netherl.**
(1) $(i_j - i_{Ger})'$	1.05	0.50	1.11	1.18	0.31
(2) s_j	-0.12	-0.06	0.10	0.04	-0.31
(3) fr_j	0.90	2.11	-2.24	0.19	4.15
(4) = (2)-(3)	-1.02	-2.17	2.34	-0.15	-4.46
(5) α = (4)/(1)	-0.97	-4.34	2.11	-0.13	-14.39

Since the management of interest rates can be used to alter the stock of foreign reserves, we also assessed the effects of a positive one-percent one-shot shock in the interest rate differential on fr_j, the domestic currency counterpart of the change in international reserves weighted by the monetary base. The resulting cumulative impulse response functions for fr_j are plotted in Figure 4.3 for a horizon of 30 months. The ultimate effects on fr_j are provided in Table 4.1, line (3).

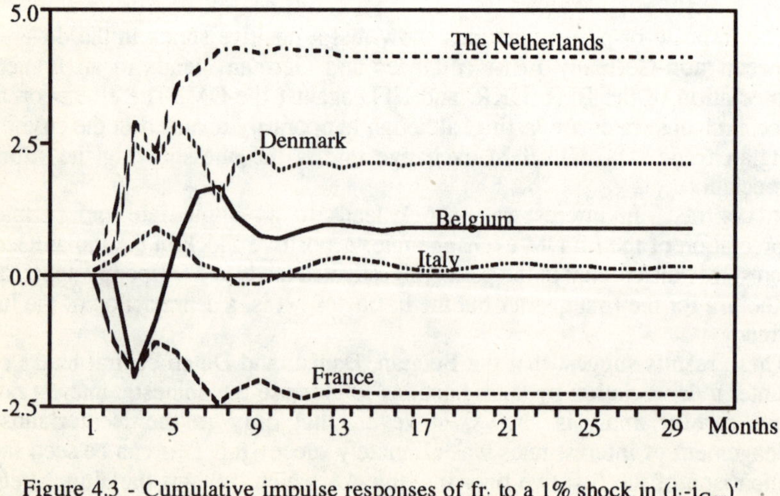

Figure 4.3 - Cumulative impulse responses of fr_j to a 1% shock in $(i_j - i_{Ger})'$

As can be seen from the impulse response functions, a positive shock in the interest rate differential leads to a quick, large and lasting increase in the stock of foreign reserves in the Netherlands and Denmark. The increase in the stock of foreign reserves is, however, largest in the Netherlands, almost twice that of Denmark. In France, a one-percent increase in $(i_{Fr}-i_{Ger})'$ leads to a quick, relatively large but lasting decrease in the stock of foreign reserves. In Italy, the initial increase in foreign reserves occurring in the first quarter dissipates in the second quarter. In Belgium, the initial loss of foreign reserves is followed by a recovery in the beginning of the second quarter and the ultimate effect on the stock of international reserves is a positive one.

From the above, it follows that if Dutch and Danish monetary authorities take unexpected actions to increase the money market interest rates, they can recover substantial amounts of international reserves. This can be seen from the comparison of lines (1) and (3) in Table 4.1. In the Netherlands, the ultimate increase in foreign reserves (relative to the monetary base) is 4.15 percent against an ultimate increase of 0.31 percent in the domestic interest rate. In Denmark, a lasting increase of 0.50 percent in the domestic interest rate leads to an increase of 2.11 percent in the stock of foreign reserves. In Belgium, a target of increasing stocks of foreign reserves requires a higher lasting increase in the interest rate than for the Netherlands and Denmark. To recover foreign reserves through unexpected increases in the domestic interest rates would not be, for the period in question, an appropriate strategy for Italy and France. In order to achieve a visible increase in the stock of international reserves an unrealistically long-lived increase in the domestic interest rate would be required in Italy. In France, an increase in the domestic interest rate would have effects which are contrary to those desired.

As noted in section 4.2, a positive innovation in the interest rate differential may, depending upon the sign of α, have a positive or negative effect on the exchange market pressure variable, (s_j-fr_j). Regardless of the sign of α, the pressure in the exchange market resulting from an innovation in the $(i_j-i_{Ger})'$ variable is shared by both the foreign reserves and the exchange rate, if the two variables move in opposite directions. As can be observed from the cumulative impulse response functions of fr_j and s_j, this has been the case for all the ERM countries except Italy.

The two last lines in Table 4.1 combine the ultimate effects on foreign reserves, exchange rates, and interest rate differentials, resulting from innovations in the interest rate differential. The figures in line (4) represent the long-run effect on the exchange market pressure variable and line (5) shows the long-run values of α from expression (4.1). It is clear that interest rate management was most effective in the Netherlands.

The high credibility of the HFL/DM central rates in the EMS is the obvious explanation for the special performance of the Netherlands. An increase in the differential between short-term interest rates for the guilder and the mark was interpreted by the market as a safe opportunity to get better returns by investing in the Dutch guilder. We return to the credibility issue in chapter 7.

[illegible] as well from the majority [illegible] a private [illegible] a position [illegible] [illegible] [illegible] in Belgium [illegible] [illegible]

We, therefore, [illegible] of Dutch and German monetary [illegible] interest [illegible] international reserves. [illegible] consumption of 10.6 [illegible] in Table 9.1 [illegible] in [illegible] increase of [illegible] per cent [illegible] in the [illegible] for the [illegible] interest rate [illegible] increase in the [illegible] appropriate [illegible] in order [illegible] the stock of international reserves [illegible] constant interest rate [illegible] an interest rate [illegible]

[illegible] monetary [illegible] dependency [illegible] the [illegible] countries [illegible]

The two [illegible] interest [illegible] the [illegible] it is clear that [illegible] Netherlands [illegible]

[illegible] the Netherlands [illegible] international [illegible] the Dutch [illegible]

CHAPTER 5
Monetary autonomy in the EMS

5.1. Introduction

In chapters 3 and 4, the ability of the members of the EMS to keep exchange rates within the margins and to attract inflows of international reserves was assessed. The analyses focused on the two instruments commonly used to immediately achieve foreign exchange targets. Our findings, combined with the realignments observed in the period under investigation, seem to indicate that the EMS left room for autonomous monetary policies. There might thus exist a vicious circle such that the independence of monetary policies in some countries might be an explanation for the inability to achieve some goals for exchange rates and stocks of foreign reserves by resorting to intervention in foreign exchange and money markets.

In contrast to this picture of relative independence, the EMS is often seen as an asymmetric system in which Germany determines its own monetary policy to which the remaining members adjust by pegging their currencies to the Deutsche mark.

This asymmetric view of the EMS has been proposed, for example, by the Commission of the European Communities (1990): "*The EMS in the 1980s could thus be characterized as an asymmetric system in which the 'centre'* [Germany], *by and large, managed its own money supply path, while the others, given unchanged bilateral rates, accepted the centre's monetary stance ... the centre systematically sterilized capital inflows, while peripheral countries, by and large, attempted to control their foreign reserves by avoiding the sterilization of capital flows.*"[41]

Despite the almost universal consensus in policy circles and among economists that monetary policy in the EMS has been dominated by the Bundesbank, empirical support for German leadership in the EMS has not been unambiguous. An illuminating example is found in Giavazzi and Giovannini (1989) who faithfully argue, on the basis of an "accounting" model, that the EMS is a DM zone. However, when the model is implemented to analyze the autonomy of the French, German, and Italian central banks, no differences between the monetary policies followed by the three countries are found.[42]

---

[41] See Commission of the European Communities (1990), page 182.

[42] The empirical rejection of the model was attributed to potential specification and data problems. See Giavazzi and Giovannini (1989), chapter 4.

The purpose of this chapter is to re-assess the asymmetry of the EMS. The analysis is separately carried out for two periods of the life of the system. The first period is the same one investigated in the two preceding chapters, i.e., a period covering the first eleven realignments. The second period is the period without realignments between 1987 and 1992. This allows us to compare the two periods and, thus, test the notion of "New EMS" described in chapter 2.

The strategy adopted in this study for assessing autonomy - like the approach based on the sterilization equation - assumes that the domestic component of the monetary base is a policy instrument at the disposal of the central banks. Our approach goes beyond a mere analysis of sterilization policies and assesses whether innovations in the domestic component of the monetary base are the result of the central bank's discretionary policy or whether they are, instead, the result of innovations in the remaining variables of the DM exchange market pressure model described in chapter 3. If the DM exchange rate constraint does not leave room for autonomous monetary policy within the EMS, then the central banks cannot use surprises in domestic credit in order to achieve internal policy targets and, therefore, most of the innovations in domestic credit are endogenously determined. In contrast, when the DM exchange rate constraint is not binding, domestic credit can be used as an instrument for pursuing domestic objectives. In this case, most of the innovations in domestic credit should not be the result of innovations in other variables but, rather, the result of innovations in the domestic credit itself. On this basis, ERM members can be ranked in terms of the degree of monetary autonomy, relative to that of Germany.

The remaining part of this chapter is organized as follows. In section 5.2 we describe the approach used in this study to assess monetary autonomy. The data is detailed in section 5.3 while section 5.4 presents the results. Finally, a summary and conclusions are presented in section 5.5.

5.2. Assessing monetary autonomy

In order to assess the constraints imposed by the DM exchange rate peg on the monetary policies in the other ERM countries, we use again the VARs described before. The degree of interdependence among the variables in a VAR can be evaluated by decomposing the variances of the forecast errors. The variance-decomposition technique is based on the moving average representation of the models and measures the contribution of each source of innovations to the variance of the n-period ahead forecast error for each variable. For our purposes, the focus is on the variance-decomposition of dc_j, the change in domestic credit, the variable of interest to assess whether a country participating in the ERM has followed a monetary policy dependent on the DM exchange rate peg. The dependence of monetary policies is evaluated as follows: If most of the innovations in dc_j are the result of innovations in the other variables from the exchange-market pressure model, we have a dependent monetary policy. When most of the innovations in dc_j are not from innovations in those variables but from independent innovations in dc_j itself, we have an independent monetary policy.

In order to provide a thorough picture of the monetary policies adopted by ERM participants, we complement the autonomy analysis with an analysis of the reaction of the money supply to innovations in the foreign reserves component of the monetary base. Instead of computing a traditional sterilization coefficient, we estimate the impulse response functions of the domestic and foreign components of the monetary base to unit shocks on the foreign reserves component, fr_j.[43] These functions trace the dynamic responses of the two variables when the system is shocked by an innovation in fr_j and all endogenous variables adjust to the new long-run equilibrium. By merging the impulse responses of dc_j with those of fr_j we obtain the net effect on the monetary base, mb_j, resulting from the initial shock in foreign reserves. This introduction of dynamics into the assessment of sterilization policies extends the traditional static analysis.

5.3. Data

The assessment of monetary autonomy of each EMS member against Germany is conducted for two separate periods. The first one extends from 1979 to 1988 and contains the first eleven realignments of the EMS. The models are exactly those used in chapters 3 and 4. The second period runs from January 1987 to August 1992, i.e., a period of stable exchange rates. The models used for the second period are similar to those used for the first one. The details on the data sources and definitions of variables in the data appendix of chapter 3 also apply to the period beginning in 1987.[44]

With the dismantling of capital controls in the beginning of the second period, the observed stability of exchange rates might be the result of higher convergence of monetary policies towards the German policy stance. If this was actually the case, one would find a decrease in the degree of monetary autonomy of the individual members. The "New EMS" would receive support under such circumstances.

[43]The analysis of sterilization in this chapter has a different point of departure from that undertaken in chapter 3. In the latter, the adjustments in the system were the result of an initial shock in the market exchange rate. In this chapter the system is assumed to be directly shocked by an innovation in foreign exchange reserves.

[44]The only exception relates to the French money stock. Due to data availability on a monthly basis, the money stock (MS) for France is *line 34* from IFS for the first period and *line 38L* for the second.
Note further that dc_j and fr_j are indexed to the beginning of each period.

5.4. Results

5.4.1. The period of realignments, 1979-1988

The variance decompositions of the innovations in dc_j for our five ERM countries are provided in Table 5.1. The results show that, in France and Italy, the innovations in the domestic credit component account for most of its own variance for all horizons. Thirty months ahead, innovations in dc_{Fr} and dc_{It} still account for more than 50 percent of own variances. These results illustrate that, for the period in question, the DM exchange rates did not bind the French and Italian monetary policies. They have not, thus, been dependent on the DM exchange rates and, therefore, on German monetary policy. The central banks of France and Italy enjoyed a large degree of monetary autonomy.

In contrast, innovations in dc have a low weight in explaining the variance of the Dutch domestic credit component. Only about 11 percent of the fluctuations in dc_{Hol} are explained by independent innovations in this variable. This is equivalent to saying that the Dutch monetary authorities did not use domestic credit in a discretionary way, but rather made it dependent on developments in the remaining relevant variables of the guilder/DM exchange market.

Belgium and Denmark are intermediate cases. While independent innovations in dc explain between 17.5 percent and 19.1 percent of the variance of the forecast errors in Belgian domestic credit, they explain between 28.4 percent and 29.6 percent of the variance in the Danish case.

Summarizing Table 5.1, the ERM countries can be ranked by the degree of monetary independence during the period:

Country	**Degree of independence**
France	64.3
Italy	54.4
Denmark	29.6
Belgium	17.5
Netherl.	11.3

This ranking for monetary independence from Germany is consistent with the pattern of DM exchange rate devaluations observed for the five currencies between 1979 and 1988.[45]

[45] A VAR model was also used by von Hagen and Fratianni (1990) to give an indication about monetary independence in the EMS during the period we have been investigating. The set of variables of the model is, however, different from ours. The strategy followed by von Hagen and Fratianni consists of assessing the impact on the individual short-term interest rates in response to interest rate innovations in each of the various members of the EMS.

Table 5.1 - Variance decomposition of domestic credit, 1979-1988

Belgium					
Proportion due to →	dc_{Bel}	fr_{Bel}	s_{Bel}	$(i_{Bel}-i_{Ger})'$	$(y_{Bel}-y_{Ger})$
2 months ahead	19.1	79.8	0.3	0.6	0.1
5 months ahead	17.6	72.5	2.3	3.1	4.6
10 months ahead	17.6	70.8	2.3	3.6	5.7
20 months ahead	17.5	70.3	2.3	3.7	6.2
30 months ahead	17.5	70.3	2.3	3.7	6.3
Denmark					
Proportion due to →	dc_{Den}	fr_{Den}	s_{Den}	$(i_{Den}-i_{Ger})'$	$(y_{Den}-y_{Ger})$
2 months ahead	28.4	68.6	1.5	0.3	1.2
5 months ahead	29.0	63.6	3.5	2.2	1.8
10 months ahead	29.5	61.8	3.7	3.1	1.9
20 months ahead	29.6	61.6	3.7	3.2	1.9
30 months ahead	29.6	61.6	3.7	3.2	1.9
France					
Proportion due to →	dc_{Fr}	fr_{Fr}	s_{Fr}	$(i_{Fr}-i_{Ger})'$	$(y_{Fr}-y_{Ger})$
2 months ahead	73.8	23.8	0.9	1.0	0.5
5 months ahead	67.3	22.8	1.1	1.8	7.1
10 months ahead	64.4	21.9	1.1	2.1	10.5
20 months ahead	64.3	21.9	1.1	2.1	10.5
30 months ahead	64.3	21.9	1.1	2.1	10.5
Italy					
Proportion due to →	dc_{It}	fr_{It}	s_{It}	$(i_{It}-i_{Ger})'$	$(y_{It}-y_{Ger})$
2 months ahead	62.7	34.2	1.5	0.2	1.4
5 months ahead	60.8	31.2	3.1	1.6	3.3
10 months ahead	55.9	35.8	3.2	1.8	3.3
20 months ahead	54.5	37.1	3.2	1.9	3.3
30 months ahead	54.4	37.1	3.2	1.9	3.4
the Netherlands					
Proportion due to →	dc_{Hol}	fr_{Hol}	s_{Hol}	$(i_{Hol}-i_{Ger})'$	$(y_{Hol}-y_{Ger})$
2 months ahead	10.5	83.4	1.6	3.1	1.3
5 months ahead	10.9	68.4	6.8	12.5	1.3
10 months ahead	11.2	66.8	7.5	12.4	2.1
20 months ahead	11.3	66.6	7.5	12.3	2.3
30 months ahead	11.3	66.6	7.5	12.3	2.3

Our results are in line with those obtained by Koedijk and Kool (1992) who, on the basis of the behavior of nominal interest rates and inflation, also investigated whether the EMS has functioned as a DM zone. These authors concluded that "*Neither for the whole period, nor for the period after March 1983 the EMS has functioned as a DM-zone. Although the Netherlands and Germany almost form one currency-area, large differences in independent interest and inflation differentials with other countries have persisted.*"

Table 5.1 also shows that the variance of dc_j which is not explained by innovations in dc_j is mostly explained by the foreign component of the monetary base, fr_j. In particular, in the Netherlands, Belgium and Denmark, the short- and long-run fluctuations of dc_j are dominated by innovations in fr_j. It is thus relevant to assess how the domestic component of the monetary base behaved in response to innovations in the foreign component.

In order to assess sterilization policies we compute the cumulative impulse responses of dc_j and fr_j to a one-percent one-shot shock in fr_j. The cumulative impulse responses of dc_j, fr_j and mb_j are plotted in Figures 5.1-5.5, for a horizon of 30 months. The mb_j cumulative impulse responses result from the algebraic sum of the responses of dc_j and fr_j. Selected values of these three functions, for different horizons, are provided in Table 5.2.

The dynamics resulting from a one-percent innovation in fr_j show that four of the five countries systematically sterilized both in the short and long run. The only exception is Denmark which, in the long run, sterilized only partially. In the Danish case, a positive shock in fr leads to an increase in fr by 0.61 percent and a rise in the monetary base by 0.27 percent.[46] This means that almost half of the final effect on foreign reserves was not sterilized.

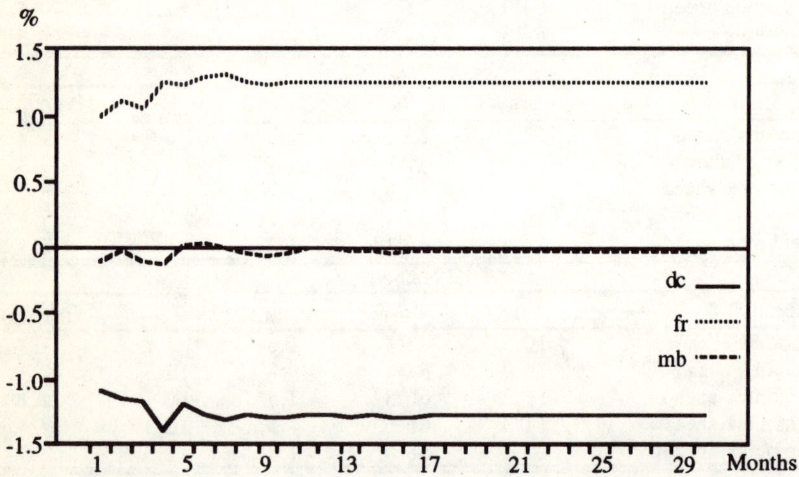

Fig. 5.1 - Cumulative responses to a 1% shock in fr, Belgium

[46]One of the criticisms that can be raised against the traditional sterilization equation is that it does not incorporate the adjustments that monetary authorities might introduce in monetary policy in the periods following the ones in which shocks in international reserves occur. This criticism receives support from the results presented here for Denmark. While the -1.04 coefficient of sterilization from the contemporaneous model would lead us to conclude that there is full sterilization, the introduction of dynamics into the analysis shows that the contemporaneous coefficient is misleading. In fact, the Danish monetary authorities allowed the innovations in foreign reserves to ultimately affect the initial money path.

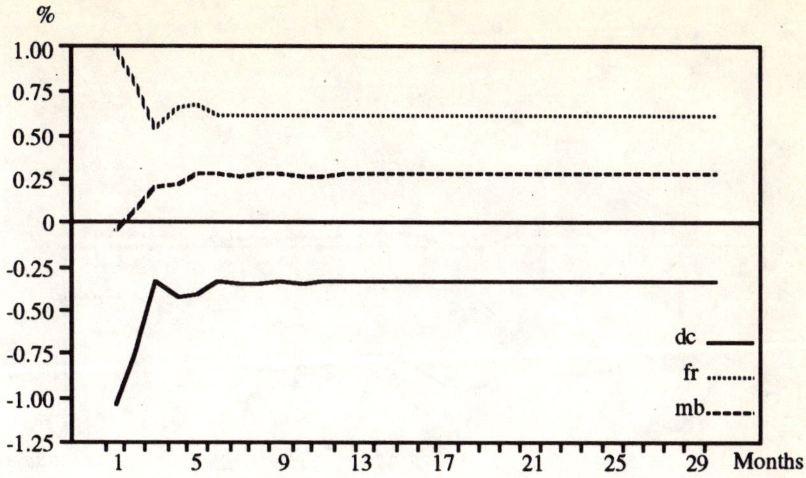

Fig. 5.2 - Cumulative responses to a 1% shock in fr, Denmark

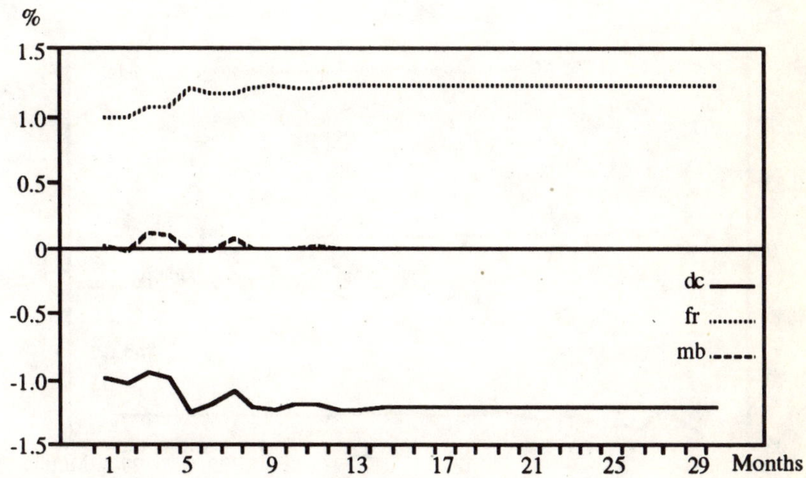

Fig. 5.3 - Cumulative responses to a 1% shock in fr, France

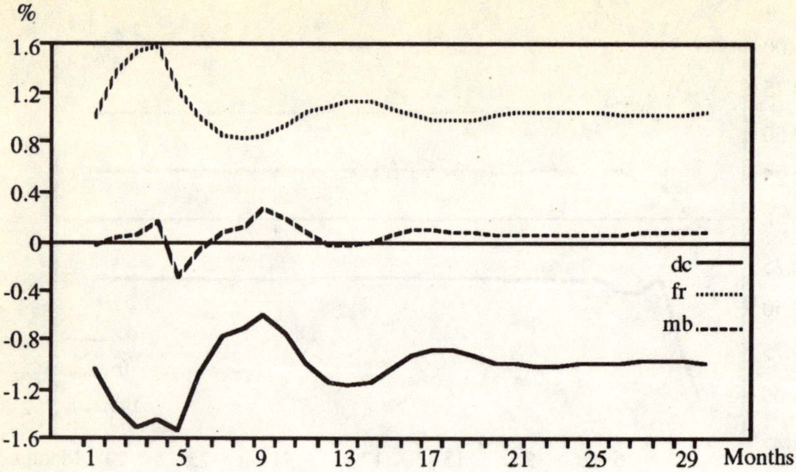

Fig. 5.4 - Cumulative responses to a 1% shock in fr, Italy

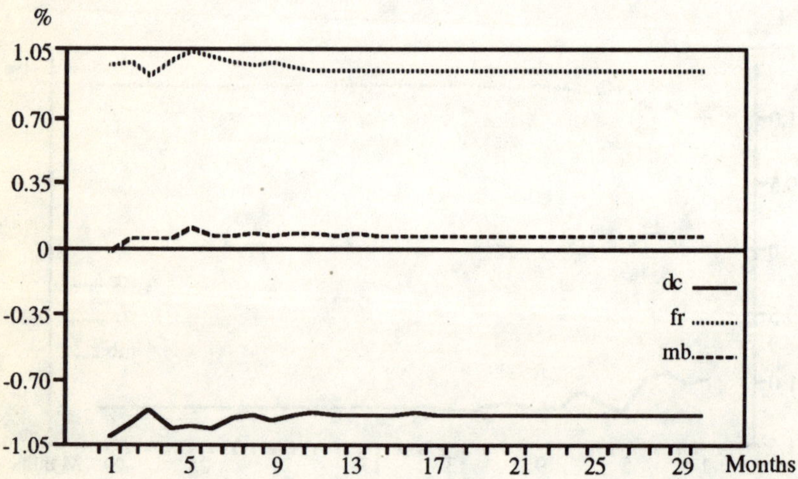

Fig. 5.5 - Cumulative responses to a 1% shock in fr, the Netherlands

Table 5.2 - Cumulative responses to a 1% shock in foreign reserves

Months		2	5	10	20	30
	fr	1.11	1.22	1.23	1.25	1.25
Belgium	dc	-1.15	-1.20	-1.29	-1.29	-1.29
	mb	-0.04	0.02	-0.06	-0.04	-0.04
	fr	0.82	0.67	0.61	0.61	0.61
Denmark	dc	-0.76	-0.40	-0.35	-0.34	-0.34
	mb	0.06	0.27	0.26	0.27	0.27
	fr	0.99	1.21	1.21	1.22	1.22
France	dc	-1.03	-1.25	-1.21	-1.22	-1.22
	mb	-0.04	-0.04	0.00	0.00	0.00
	fr	1.37	1.23	0.95	1.02	1.04
Italy	dc	-1.34	-1.53	-0.76	-0.97	-0.98
	mb	0.03	-0.30	0.19	0.05	0.06
	fr	0.99	1.04	0.96	0.95	0.95
Netherl.	dc	-0.94	-0.94	-0.88	-0.88	-0.88
	mb	0.05	0.10	0.08	0.07	0.07

Among the remaining countries, only in Italy and the Netherlands does a positive shock in fr lead to a long-run increase in the monetary base, although only a small one. Thus, the impulse response functions show that Denmark was the only ERM member which allowed changes in the stock of foreign reserves to affect domestic money growth. In contrast, the Belgian, French, Italian and Dutch central banks systematically defended their money supplies against shocks in the foreign reserves component.

5.4.2. The "New EMS", 1987-1992

The variance decompositions of the forecast errors in dc_j in the period between January 1987 and August 1992 are provided in Table 5.3.

As before, the results can be summarized by ranking the countries in terms of monetary autonomy:

Country	Degree of independence
Denmark	57.3
Netherl.	43.8
France	40.7
Italy	40.5
Belgium	15.0

Table 5.3 - Variance decomposition of domestic credit, 1987-1992

Belgium					
Proportion due to →	dc_{Bel}	fr_{Bel}	s_{Bel}	$(i_{Bel}-i_{Ger})'$	$(y_{Bel}-y_{Ger})$
2 months ahead	18.4	56.2	19.9	1.1	4.4
5 months ahead	15.2	50.7	18.8	6.5	8.8
10 months ahead	15.2	45.4	24.0	7.4	8.0
20 months ahead	15.0	44.5	24.0	7.7	8.8
30 months ahead	15.0	44.4	24.0	7.7	8.9
Denmark					
Proportion due to →	dc_{Den}	fr_{Den}	s_{Den}	$(i_{Den}-i_{Ger})'$	$(y_{Den}-y_{Ger})$
2 months ahead	74.3	23.9	0.5	0.2	1.1
5 months ahead	59.5	24.3	1.0	12.7	2.5
10 months ahead	57.4	23.3	2.1	13.9	3.3
20 months ahead	57.3	23.3	2.1	13.9	3.4
30 months ahead	57.3	23.3	2.1	13.9	3.4
France					
Proportion due to →	dc_{Fr}	fr_{Fr}	s_{Fr}	$(i_{Fr}-i_{Ger})'$	$(y_{Fr}-y_{Ger})$
2 months ahead	71.7	22.5	1.2	2.6	2.0
5 months ahead	44.1	14.1	22.7	10.3	8.8
10 months ahead	42.5	13.7	22.2	12.4	9.2
20 months ahead	40.8	13.2	23.0	13.1	9.9
30 months ahead	40.7	13.2	23.0	13.2	9.9
Italy					
Proportion due to →	dc_{It}	fr_{It}	s_{It}	$(i_{It}-i_{Ger})'$	$(y_{It}-y_{Ger})$
2 months ahead	50.4	46.0	1.7	0.5	1.4
5 months ahead	42.3	36.3	10.5	7.7	3.2
10 months ahead	40.5	36.8	11.2	7.7	3.8
20 months ahead	40.5	36.5	11.2	7.9	3.9
30 months ahead	40.5	36.5	11.2	7.9	3.9
the Netherlands					
Proportion due to →	dc_{Hol}	fr_{Hol}	s_{Hol}	$(i_{Hol}-i_{Ger})'$	$(y_{Hol}-y_{Ger})$
2 months ahead	81.0	8.3	0.5	3.0	7.2
5 months ahead	52.4	6.4	2.5	6.6	32.1
10 months ahead	47.0	6.1	4.0	16.3	26.6
20 months ahead	43.9	6.1	5.5	18.6	25.9
30 months ahead	43.8	6.2	5.6	18.6	25.8

The results are quite different from those obtained for the period of frequent realignments. It is clear that France and Italy lost part of the monetary independence they had enjoyed in the first period. In both countries, less than 50 percent of the innovations in dc_j are the result of independent policies in the second period. In contrast, the results for Denmark and the Netherlands point to the opposite direction. Independent innovations of dc_j doubled their contribution in Denmark while in the Netherlands their contribution increased from 11.3 to 43.8

percent. In Belgium, the degree of autonomy of dc_j is practically the same in the two periods.

Given the stability of EMS exchange rates in the more recent period, the results seem surprising. They suggest that, with the exception of Belgium, a great deal of the innovations in dc_j are the result of autonomous monetary policies relative to that followed by Germany. While one would expect greater convergence to the German policy stance, what we actually find is greater divergence of monetary policies. A possible explanation for these results has to do with how convergence can be achieved.

Convergence of monetary policies in a fixed exchange rate regime can be made towards a low- or a high-inflation standard. What we have been implicitly assuming is that Germany is the low inflation country to which the other countries try to converge. Such an assumption is not, however, valid for the whole period between 1987 and 1992. Inflation pressures following German unification disqualified this country as the best inflation performer in the EMS. The most likely reason for the results found for the period between 1987 and 1992 is, thus, that the divergence was consciously assumed by EMS members; they might have tried to achieve inflation targets which were lower than inflation rates actually observed in Germany.[47]

Given the above observation, we shorten our second sample to January 1987 until May 1990. Variance decompositions of dc_j for this narrow period are presented in Table 5.4. The results are quite different from those obtained when the sample was extended until August 1992.

In the five countries, a small percentage of the innovations in dc_j are now the result of independent policies. Relative to the findings for the period of frequent realignments, monetary autonomy has clearly decreased in all EMS members. The only exception are the Netherlands. The ranking of the countries in terms of the degree of monetary autonomy, relative to Germany, is summarized below. It shows that Belgian monetary policy became the least autonomous one between 1987 and 1990 while the degree of autonomy in the remaining countries is also low and quite similar to each other.

Country	Degree of independence
Denmark	18.3
Netherl.	17.9
France	17.6
Italy	16.6
Belgium	8.4

[47] This reasoning fits together with the conclusions of Gardner and Perraudin (1993) who found that, following unification, Germany lost its leadership role within the EMS.

Table 5.4 - Variance decomposition of domestic credit, 1987-1990

Belgium					
Proportion due to →	dc_{Bel}	fr_{Bel}	s_{Bel}	$(i_{Bel}-i_{Ger})'$	$(y_{Bel}-y_{Ger})$
2 months ahead	16.8	30.3	1.1	0.5	51.3
5 months ahead	13.5	36.0	2.8	16.1	31.6
10 months ahead	13.8	29.4	7.4	19.1	30.3
20 months ahead	11.4	27.0	8.2	29.1	24.3
30 months ahead	8.4	26.1	6.1	41.1	18.3
Denmark					
Proportion due to →	dc_{Den}	fr_{Den}	s_{Den}	$(i_{Den}-i_{Ger})'$	$(y_{Den}-y_{Ger})$
2 months ahead	29.2	34.0	1.7	5.3	29.8
5 months ahead	19.0	32.8	6.8	18.7	22.7
10 months ahead	18.5	30.3	7.3	16.9	27.0
20 months ahead	18.3	28.7	10.0	15.9	27.1
30 months ahead	18.3	28.5	10.2	15.8	27.2
France					
Proportion due to →	dc_{Fr}	fr_{Fr}	s_{Fr}	$(i_{Fr}-i_{Ger})'$	$(y_{Fr}-y_{Ger})$
2 months ahead	49.4	32.5	5.8	3.5	8.8
5 months ahead	22.4	22.5	33.0	12.3	9.8
10 months ahead	21.5	15.7	23.2	10.9	28.7
20 months ahead	18.6	13.5	23.8	13.6	30.5
30 months ahead	17.6	11.7	24.9	14.1	31.7
Italy					
Proportion due to →	dc_{It}	fr_{It}	s_{It}	$(i_{It}-i_{Ger})'$	$(y_{It}-y_{Ger})$
2 months ahead	34.3	47.2	11.6	1.8	5.1
5 months ahead	25.7	50.6	7.8	9.5	6.4
10 months ahead	22.3	45.6	10.4	15.7	6.0
20 months ahead	19.4	48.8	9.5	16.0	6.3
30 months ahead	16.6	52.5	8.6	16.3	6.0
the Netherlands					
Proportion due to →	dc_{Hol}	fr_{Hol}	s_{Hol}	$(i_{Hol}-i_{Ger})'$	$(y_{Hol}-y_{Ger})$
2 months ahead	48.5	30.2	9.5	3.6	8.2
5 months ahead	34.3	19.0	10.4	25.8	10.5
10 months ahead	21.2	19.0	12.4	34.4	13.0
20 months ahead	18.3	18.6	13.3	35.4	14.4
30 months ahead	17.9	18.8	13.3	35.3	14.7

5.5. Summary and conclusions

The main purpose of this chapter was to assess to what extent the monetary policies adopted by the non-Germany ERM countries have been dependent on the DM exchange market. The analysis was conducted for two periods: a period containing the first eleven realignments of the EMS and a more stable one where central parities were kept fixed.

To assess the monetary autonomy of EMS members relative to Germany, the methodology adopted in this chapter focused on domestic credit but from a different perspective than the one adopted in the traditional sterilization equations. The underlying reasoning behind our strategy is that in an asymmetric exchange regime of fixed rates monetary authorities in small countries cannot use domestic credit to achieve domestic objectives. Most of the innovations in domestic credit should, therefore, be the result of innovations in the relevant foreign exchange market variables rather than the result of active monetary policies. On the contrary, the more a country enjoys monetary autonomy, the more the innovations in domestic credit would be the result of discretionary behavior. To explore this idea, we have used VAR estimations for a set of variables from the DM exchange market pressure model described in chapter 3. The degree of the use of domestic credit as a policy instrument was assessed through the forecast variance decomposition technique. In comparison to other studies on German leadership in the EMS, an advantage of our methodology is that it allows for ranking the countries by the degree of monetary independence from that followed by Germany.

The results from the variance decomposition show that, in the period from 1979 to 1988, both France and Italy followed relatively autonomous monetary policies. Domestic credit in the two countries was used as an independent policy instrument. The claimed asymmetry of the EMS was not confirmed neither for France nor for Italy. At the other extreme is the Netherlands, which lost the independence of monetary policy. Denmark and Belgium are intermediate cases.

While - given the stability of the DM exchange rates - one would expect less autonomy in the period from 1987 to 1992, the results for some of the countries turn out to show the opposite. The explanation for this is that, with German unification, inflation in Germany lost its role as the standard to which the others should converge. Some of the countries might have pursued independent policies in relation to Germany with the purpose of obtaining lower inflation rates. This is confirmed through the results found for the period between 1987 and 1990. In this period, domestic monetary policies in EMS countries have been in line with those observed in Germany. This was, thus, a period of convergence of policies in the EMS.

On the whole, the comparison of the results for the periods from 1979 to 1988 and from 1987 to 1990 give support to the idea of a "New EMS".

These results pave the way for the next chapters. They seem to question the celebrated "EMS discipline/credibility hypotheses". The main idea behind these hypotheses is that by joining the EMS, a country joins a system of fixed exchange rates and, therefore, its hands become tied with regard to the pursuit of independent monetary policies. Since private agents are aware of this, the credibility of monetary authorities improves with participation in the EMS. As a result, the costs of disinflation are lower than when disinflationary policies are undertaken outside the system. It is often claimed that the motivation for the inflation-prone countries to join the system was just to borrow Bundesbank's anti-inflation reputation. However, the fact that France and Italy actively used monetary policies after joining the EMS does not seem to conform with the discipline/credibility view. The question of whether the EMS has improved the credibility of the French and Italian monetary authorities is discussed in the next two chapters.

CHAPTER 6
The discipline hypothesis: What role for the EMS?

6.1. Introduction

The reduction and convergence of inflation rates experienced by the members of the European Monetary System was a feature of the 1980s. This is shown in Figure 6.1 which displays (annualized) monthly inflation rates for Belgium, Denmark, France, Germany, Italy, and the Netherlands, for the period from March 1979 to December 1992.

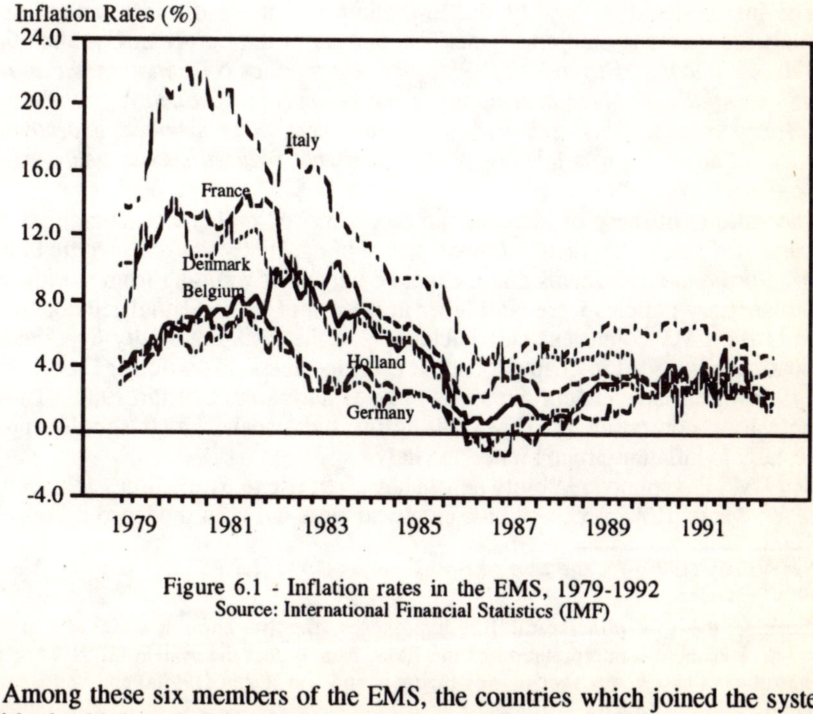

Figure 6.1 - Inflation rates in the EMS, 1979-1992
Source: International Financial Statistics (IMF)

Among these six members of the EMS, the countries which joined the system with the highest inflation rates were Italy, France, and Denmark, with 13.0

percent, 10.2 percent, and 7.2 percent, respectively. The Dutch, Belgian, and German rates of inflation were, by that time, close to each other and relatively low. In all countries, the inflation rates increased after the launching of the EMS and peaked between mid-1980 and mid-1982. Thereafter, there was a generalized disinflationary trend until 1986. This trend led, for some time, to negative inflation rates in Germany and the Netherlands. By the middle of 1988, the inflation rates in all the six countries were below the 5 percent level.

The two stylized facts within the EMS, inflation reduction and convergence, led some to conclude that those achievements were due to the operation of the system. Two inter-related hypotheses were born: the *EMS discipline hypothesis* and the *EMS credibility hypothesis*. These hypotheses have been advanced to explain why inflation-prone countries like France and Italy have adhered to the system right from the beginning. More recently, the same type of arguments has been used by EMS supporters to justify full participation of the inflation-prone newcomers, Spain and Portugal, and Greece which remains outside the system.[48]

The *EMS discipline hypothesis* can be stated as follows: assuming that the EMS imposes limitations on exchange rate fluctuations and that the inflation-averse Germany is the center of the system, a country which is traditionally prone to inflation and decides to join the EMS becomes automatically subject to monetary discipline. The *EMS credibility hypothesis* follows immediately: the reputation acquired through EMS discipline enables monetary authorities to credibly announce disinflationary programs such that the resulting output costs are lower than if a similar policy had been undertaken outside the system.[49]

The instrumentalist view of the EMS, implicit in the discipline/credibility hypotheses, is made explicit by the Commission of the European Communities (1990) as follows: "*Through the 1980s, monetary policy coordination within the EMS essentially involved acceptance of the key currency standard by the other ERM members: via this exchange-rate commitment, other members expected to reduce inflation towards low levels at a somewhat reduced cost in below-trend economic activity.*"[50]

The validity of these hypotheses can be questioned on two accounts. First, as documented below, the disinflationary stance of the 1980s was not specific to the EMS. Furthermore, it seems that the real activity costs resulting from worldwide disinflationary policies were not higher in the rest of the industrialized countries than in the EMS countries. This is contrary to the EMS credibility hypothesis. Second, as discussed in chapter 5, some EMS members, in particular France and Italy, followed independent monetary policies during most of the 1980s. Those conclusions contradict the EMS discipline hypothesis which should apply especially to inflation-prone France and Italy.

The EMS discipline/credibility debate has given rise to lively discussions in the past few years. However, very little empirical work has been produced in support

[48]See Viñals (1990) for the case of Spain, Torres (1990) for Portugal and Papademos (1990) for Greece.

[49]Besides the discipline/credibility hypotheses, the literature has developed an alternative economic interpretation of the EMS, namely that the system might work as an absorber of exogenous shocks [See Fratianni and von Hagen (1990a) and von Hagen (1993)].

[50]See Commission of the European Communities (1990), page 182.

of the hypotheses. This might be a result of the difficulty of translating concepts like "discipline" and "credibility" into a straightforward measure. Despite the fact that the monetary discipline/credibility hypotheses involve dynamic relationships between money supply, inflation, exchange rates and output, most empirical studies have focused on a single variable, the inflation rate.

The fact that the design of the EMS allows for realignments questions the anti-inflationary role of the system. However, the observation that at realignments high-inflation countries did not ask for full recovery of competitiveness leads to a re-interpretation of the discipline hypothesis: active monetary policies in the EMS may in practice have perverse effects due to exchange rate constraints [Minford (1989), Hughes-Hallett *et al.* (1990) and De Grauwe (1990)]. This would constitute a mechanism to refrain from activism. The purpose of this chapter is to investigate whether the EMS has operated as an arrangement that, through self-imposed exchange rate rigidity, weakens the incentives for expansionary monetary policies.[51]

This chapter is organized as follows. In section 6.2 we describe how the disciplinary role of the EMS has been formally put forward in the literature. Some theoretical problems with the EMS discipline hypothesis are raised in section 6.3. A review of empirical studies produced on the EMS discipline/credibility hypotheses is provided in section 6.4. Section 6.5 contains the record of the unemployment/inflation trade-off for a set of EMS and non-EMS countries. A strategy for analysing the role of the exchange rate in monetary authorities' incentives is suggested and applied to Italy and France in section 6.6. Section 6.7 presents a summary and conclusions.

6.2. The "tying-one's-hands" model of discipline

The way that the EMS may impose discipline to the members and, thereby, deliver credibility, is formally modelled in Giavazzi and Pagano's (1988) well-known paper "The advantage of tying one's hands - EMS discipline and central bank credibility". The model is based on the problem of time-consistent policies discussed by Kydland and Prescott (1977), Calvo (1978) and Barro and Gordon (1983a). Giavazzi and Pagano present an extension to an open economy of the model of Barro and Gordon (1983b) which can be described as follows.[52]

The objective of the policymaker is the maximization of a utility function, z_t, in each period. This function is given by

$$z_t = a\,(e_t - \pi_t) + b\,(\pi_t - \pi_t^e) - \frac{c}{2}\,\pi_t^2 \tag{6.1}$$

---

[51]The hypothesis raised here implicitly assumes that there might be intentional asymmetry in the EMS. Wyplosz (1989) considers that asymmetry in the EMS is systemic rather than the result of self-imposed constraints by non-Germany EMS countries. Russo and Tullio (1988) and Giovannini (1989) discuss the two hypotheses.

[52]For a broad survey of studies on credibility concerning inflation and other aspects of macroeconomic policy see Persson (1987).

where *a*, *b*, and *c* are positive parameters; e_t is the change in the nominal exchange rate while π_t and π^e_t are, respectively, domestic inflation and expectations of domestic inflation formed one period in advance. The nominal exchange rate is defined as the number of domestic currency units per unit of foreign currency. Foreign prices are, for simplicity, assumed constant and, therefore, the change in the real exchange rate is given by $(e_t-\pi_t)$. Wage rates prevailing during period t are assumed to be set at the end of period t-1. It is assumed that the economy is growing at its natural rate and, accordingly, wage rates are set at the rate of inflation expected for t, that is, at π^e_t.

The first two terms on the right-hand side of equation (6.1) take into account that two types of goods are produced. One good is domestically sold while the other is exported. It is further assumed that firms manage the price of domestic goods and are pricetakers in the international goods markets. The term $[a(e_t-\pi_t)]$ shows that the policymaker is concerned with the balance of payments or, equivalently, the export-oriented sector. *Ceteris paribus*, an increase in inflation worsens the current account. The incentive to create surprise inflation and, thereby, increase the production of the domestically consumed good is captured by $[b(\pi_t-\pi^e_t)]$. A decrease in real wages and the resulting higher net profits provide firms with an incentive to produce more. Since the parameters *a* and *b* are positive, a real exchange rate appreciation would imply a decrease in the monetary authorities' utility, while a level of actual inflation higher than the agreed wage rate would provide policymakers with more utility. Finally, the monetary authorities dislike price instability and, accordingly, $[(c/2)\pi^2_t]$ has a negative sign.[53]

The policymaker aims at maximizing his objective function and, for that matter, controls a monetary instrument that enables him to select the rate of inflation in each period. The optimal solution for the model would be, regardless of the exchange rate regime, a rate of inflation equal to zero. The optimal solution is not, however, time-consistent. With wage inflation set equal to zero, monetary authorities are tempted to inflate. The game between the policymaker and the wage setters must thus lead to an equilibrium where such a possibility is discarded and the expectations of wage setters are fulfilled. The only credible monetary policy is one that does not affect output growth. Thus, output will equal its natural rate and inflation becomes unnecessarily high in the time-consistent equilibrium. The lower the weight that monetary authorities give to inflation in the utility function, the higher the time-consistent equilibrium rate of inflation.

According to Giavazzi and Pagano, the time-consistent solution, call it π_t*, depends upon the exchange rate regime. To illustrate the advantages of participating in the EMS they consider two polar situations, one of fixed rates which is identified with the EMS, and another of freely floating exchange rates where purchasing power parity (PPP) is assumed to hold.[54] In both exchange rate

[53] In countries with high public debt, monetary authorities may like to obtain seigniorage revenues and reduce the real value of the debt through the ensuing inflation. In this case, a positive term for inflation should be included in the utility function. This issue is discussed in the context of EMS discipline by, for example, Giavazzi (1989), Grilli (1989) and Gros (1990).

[54] Henceforth the subscripts EMS and PPP will identify the situation which we are referring to.

regimes the reference currency is the DM which serves the purpose of pegging to a low inflation country.

Given rational expectations, private agents can predict inflation by solving out the policymaker's optimization problem. Maximization of expression (6.1) with respect to inflation leads to

$$\pi^*_{t,EMS} = \frac{b - a}{c} \qquad (6.2.a)$$

and

$$\pi^*_{t,PPP} = \frac{b}{c} \qquad (6.2.b)$$

that is, although output growth does not deviate from its natural rate, a lower inflation rate is obtained under the EMS, compared with the regime of freely floating exchange rates.[55,56] Solutions (6.2.a) and (6.2.b) show the advantage of *tying one's hands* and how the EMS exchange rate regime may help member countries with high inflation to achieve a better performance. The decrease in the equilibrium inflation rates is due to the penalty that the EMS regime attaches to inflationary policies which involve the deterioration of the current account. It is via the constraints imposed by the external sector that the EMS disciplinary role is supposed to work for the inflation-prone members: wage setters are assumed to internalize the welfare costs of real exchange rate appreciations that monetary authorities would bear if they carry out expansionary monetary policies.

In terms of the policymaker's utility function, the maximization problem leads to a less negative outcome in the EMS regime since part of the disutility found under the PPP regime is eliminated. Maximization of (6.1) leads to

$$z^*_{t,EMS} = -\frac{b^2}{2c} + \frac{a^2}{2c} \qquad (6.3.a)$$

and

$$z^*_{t,PPP} = -\frac{b^2}{2c} \qquad (6.3.b)$$

for the fixed and the floating exchange rate regimes, respectively. Although a non-cooperative game between wage setters and monetary authorities is assumed to be played in the two regimes, the EMS outcome is closer to the solution under a cooperative game. Given (6.3.a) and (6.3.b), Giavazzi and Pagano (1988) conclude that the EMS *is a welfare-improving arrangement from the viewpoint of the monetary authorities* of high-inflation countries.

For explanatory purposes it is assumed that the parameters *a*, *b*, and *c* are independent of the exchange rate system. These parameters need not, however, be the same under fixed and flexible exchange rate regimes (the slope of the Phillips curve, for example, is not necessarily the same across different exchange rate regimes). See Glick and Wihlborg (1990).

[55] Positive correlation between money supply and inflation implies b>a.

[56] As in this section, most of the literature dealing with models of discipline/credibility provides only the equilibrium solution. Wihlborg and Willett (1990) is one of the few studies which analyze the dynamics driving the economy to the equilibrium solution.

6.3. Some theoretical problems with the EMS discipline hypothesis

6.3.1. Is the EMS time-consistent?

If, in the fixed exchange rate regime (i.e., the EMS), wage growth is set at the value given by expression (6.2.a), the monetary authorities have an incentive to create surprise inflation. Once wage rates are agreed to for the next period, the utility function of the monetary authorities is given by

$$z_t = a\,(e_t - \pi_t) + b\,(\pi_t - \frac{b-a}{c}) - \frac{c}{2}\pi_t^2 \qquad (6.4)$$

The welfare given by (6.3.a) can be improved by creating inflation in an amount greater than that given by [(b-a)/c] and either asking for a realignment in order to keep PPP constant or leaving the system.[57] Maximization of (6.4) under these circumstances leads to an optimal inflation rate given by b/c which, in turn, provides the authorities with utility amounting to

$$-\frac{b^2}{2c} + \frac{2ab}{2c}$$

This level of utility, which is higher than the utility given by (6.3.a),[58] shows that the solution (6.2.a) is not time-consistent. With respect to inflation, the EMS and the PPP exchange rate regimes are, thus, not distinguishable from each other. Whatever the true intentions of the authorities are when they join the system, the time-consistent solution is the same in both regimes.

In order to overcome this criticism, Giavazzi and Giovannini (1988) and Mélitz (1988) argue that devaluations and/or the abandonment of the system have political costs attached to them. The idea is that a devaluation in a fixed exchange rate system is interpreted by voters not as a market outcome but rather as a failure of the government. Knowing this, the government would have an additional incentive to pursue the monetary policies that are consistent with pegging. Empirical support for this argument is, however, to be found.

Note, further, that the solution found for the EMS is not sustainable in the long run since a loss of foreign reserves amounting to [(a-b)/c] occurs every period. EMS membership cannot prevail in the long run. Giavazzi and Pagano solve this problem by imposing realignments which set the real exchange rate above PPP in an amount equal to the average loss of competitiveness between two consecutive changes in the central parities. Accordingly, the two authors consider that the increase in the length of the interval between realignments reinforces the disciplinary role of the system since the policymaker would have an additional

[57] The destabilizing effects of exchange rate escape clauses, especially realignments, are analyzed in detail by Obstfeld (1991).

[58] As noted in a footnote above, positive correlation between money supply and inflation implies b>a. It follows that $2ab>a^2$.

reason to commit himself in advance to a rule for determining inflation.[59] With realignments totally forbidden, the constraints on the balance of payments would eventually lead to full convergence of inflation among EMS members and central banks and the system would be fully credible. However, if lengthening the interval between realignments gives rise to lower expected inflation, the temptation to create surprise inflation is higher since the utility that can be derived from such a behavior is also higher.

6.3.2. The alternatives to exchange rate pegging

As pointed out by Begg (1988), the EMS discipline hypothesis does not explain why it is better to target the exchange rate when the primary goal is to reduce the inflation rate. For this purpose, management of the money supply would seem the most appropriate and direct strategy. If the authorities are really commited to lower inflation, a solution would be, for example, to have an independent central bank and to appoint a *"conservative"* central banker [Rogoff (1985a)]. When the goal is to reduce inflation, adopting an exchange rate target is, in principle, equivalent to adopting a money supply target: if the money supply is taken as exogenous, the exchange rate becomes endogenous, and vice-versa. The ability of the monetary authorities to convince people of the seriousness of an anti-inflationary policy is more important than the exchange rate regime in which such a policy is intended. Governments with good reputation do not need anything more than the announcement of an anti-inflationary program. Instead of by participation in the EMS, disinflation could thus be achieved by an institutional reform which replaces politically dependent monetary authorities with authorities which are primarily concerned with price stability.[60]

Besides the lack of an explanation of why is it better to peg the exchange rate than to appoint a "conservative" central banker, there might be a superior alternative to the EMS as a source of discipline. As pointed out by De Grauwe (1990), joining the EMS might not be the best choice if the primary purpose of a country is to disinflate. De Grauwe argues that monetary authorities can follow one of two strategies to reestablish reputation: "gradualism" or "shock therapy". In the latter case, monetary authorities seek to convince the public that they are hard on inflation. To this end, they contract the money supply and force a recession. By adopting, alternatively, a gradualist strategy, the monetary authorities can avoid deep recessions but need more time to slow down inflationary expectations. De Grauwe notes that while countries outside the EMS, particularly the U.K. and the U.S., adopted shock therapies in the beginning of the 1980s in order to reestablish a good reputation, such strategies were not at the disposal of the members of the EMS with reputational problems.

---

[59] In the same line, Mélitz (1988) also asserts that *"lengthening the interval between realignments can enhance ... monetary discipline"*. See Mélitz (1988), proposition 5, page 67.

[60] The link between political dependence of central banks and inflation performance is evaluated by, for example, Alesina (1989).

6.3.3. The role of foreign exchange controls

Another problem with the discipline hypothesis is that the use of foreign exchange controls is required to make the EMS sustainable.[61] The reason is that, since realignments are periodically necessary to recover international competitiveness, central banks would be often subject to speculative attacks. The only way to avoid large outflows of foreign reserves under such circumstances is the introduction of restrictions on the free movement of capital. However, such barriers create distortions in the the economy. In countries where policymakers are strongly averse to capital controls, the use of the EMS to disinflate is out of the question.

6.3.4. How do we explain German participation in the EMS?

In the model above it was assumed that the center of the system (Germany) has zero inflation, its monetary authorities do not have any other target than price stability and they do not react to the policies adopted by the remaining partners. However, if German inflation is positive and is the outcome of a similar monetary policy game, the time-consistent policy in Germany reacts to the fact that EMS members peg to the Deutsche mark. In this case, Germany ends up with an inflation rate which is higher than without the EMS.[62]

This implies that Germany, with the role of anchor of the system, loses from participation in the EMS. This raises the question, why is Germany in the EMS? The EMS discipline hypothesis is not able to provide an appropriate answer.

Some reasons have been suggested to justify German membership and, through it, preserve the EMS discipline hypothesis. One is that the Bundesbank has no credibility problem in the first place so that German equilibrium inflation is zero with and without the EMS. In this case, the Bundesbank would be indifferent about the EMS. However, as von Hagen (1993) notes, this does not fit together with the strong opposition of the German central bank to the formation of the system. Fratianni (1988), in turn, notes that the Bundesbank may lose from the EMS but cannot do anything about it since participation was a political decision of the government. Branson (1988) complements this view and notes: "*Perhaps the answer is not to be found within the limited sphere of economic policy, but rather in the international politics of Europe. The EMS is one part of a system of unifying structures in Western Europe; presumably Germany gains from this system of unification overall, even if it does not benefit from the EMS in particular*". Mélitz's (1988) and De Cecco's (1989) explanations for German participation in the EMS are that Germany exchanges higher inflation for a better competitive position of its industries. Von Hagen (1993) argues that these

[61] See, for example, Driffill (1988), Obstfeld (1988) and Giavazzi (1989). Gros (1992) argues in contrast that capital controls were not relevant for the stability of the EMS.

[62] This can be shown through a simple two-country model of the type of Canzoneri and Henderson (1988) and Fratianni and von Hagen (1990a,b,c,d).

mercantilistic views imply unsustainable, persistent trade imbalances.[63] Fratianni and von Hagen (1990b) and von Hagen (1993) assert that the Bundesbank, although losing in terms of inflation, might be interested in the EMS in order to spread across the participating countries the speculative pressures originating from the U.S. dollar market.[64] Since, in high-inflation members of the EMS, currency restrictions were eliminated only in the end of the 1980s, this explanation implies that Germany was willing to bear the costs (higher inflation) first, with the prospects of achieving the benefits (capital mobility) later.

6.4. The EMS discipline/credibility hypotheses: Empirical evidence

As discussed above, the discipline mechanism of the EMS is supposed to work through four variables and in the following way: an increase in the money supply leads to inflation and real exchange rate appreciation. The exchange rate appreciation leads, in turn, to a decrease in output growth. This mechanism prevents the use of inflationary policies. Despite the fact that the theoretical arguments consider the inter-relations between all the four variables, the behavior of inflation rates in EMS countries has, for most researchers, narrowed the focus to a partial analysis of prices only.

Analytical strategies exclusively based on prices essentially try to verify whether the EMS helps to explain inflation rates in the member countries. Artis and Nachane (1990) assessed whether expectations about German inflation help to forecast inflation expectations in other EMS countries and in a non-EMS control country, the U.K. They found that the EMS "*offered its members a direct route to the German Standard*". According to these findings, a country acquires the credibility of German monetary authorities by joining the EMS. The idea that the EMS may have helped high inflation countries to reduce inflationary expectations was also explored by Kremers (1990) for the case of Ireland. The conclusion is that expectations on Irish inflation have adjusted towards the EMS stance or, equivalently, that the system provided Ireland with credibility in the pursuit of disinflationary policies.

The opposite conclusions were drawn by Collins (1988) who also focused exclusively on the behavior of inflation rates. Collins found evidence of a decrease in inflation after 1979 for the industrialized countries as a whole but no evidence for a special decrease among EMS members. According to these results, the EMS did not help in reducing inflation rates.[65] Artis and Nachane (1990) also conducted cointegration tests on inflation. If the EMS forces inflation in the member countries to adjust to the German standard, one would expect cointegration

[63]According to Blanchard and Muet (1993), the recent French macroeconomic strategy is based on a similar mercantilistic view.

[64]For a related discussion, see Giavazzi and Giovannini (1986).

[65]The study of Collins (1988) overcomes the drawback of the study by Ungerer *et al.* (1986) who made a similar analysis but did not assess whether the inflation shift in 1979 also applies to the non-EMS group of countries.

between German inflation and inflation in the remaining EMS member countries after 1979. This should not, however, apply before 1979. Furthermore, the German standard should not apply to the non-EMS control country either. However, their cointegration tests did not support the EMS discipline hypothesis.[66]

The latter results make clear that disinflation has been a feature of the *EMS period* but *not* specific to the *EMS arrangement.* The disinflation of the 1980s reflects a worldwide reaction to the high inflation rates prevailing in the preceding years. Figure 6.1, above, also suggests the following question: if disinflation in France and Italy in the 1980s was due to pegging the DM, what explains the disinflation in Germany? Furthermore, the disinflationary performance in Germany was not not worse than that of the high-inflation-EMS countries who tied their currencies to the DM. This can be seen from the ratios of French and Italian inflation rates to the corresponding German rates. These ratios are plotted in Figure 6.2 and show a quite stable relation during the period of disinflation, meaning that the relative performance of high-inflation countries did not improve during the 1980s.[67]

A related explanation of the behavior of inflation rates during the 1980s relies on the behavior of international oil prices. Figures 6.3.a and 6.3.b show that the (U.S. dollar) prices of oil moved close to the inflation rates in Italy and France. High correlation between inflation rates of these two countries may thus be a direct result of shocks in oil prices.

Furthermore, the two diagrams question the idea that the monetary authorities in countries which joined the system with high inflation rates needed two or three years to start benefitting from Bundesbank's reputation [Kremers (1990)]. This period seems to correspond, instead, to the effects resulting from the oil shock which occurred at the time of the EMS inception. The plot of a similar diagram for the U.K. supports this line of reasoning. Figure 6.3.c shows that British inflation also increased substantially during 1979 and 1980. The fact that the U.K., although not benefitting from alleged EMS credibility, was nevertheless able to start its disinflationary process earlier than France and Italy is noteworthy. Furthermore, the United Kingdom reached a state of low inflation much faster!

In sum, what should be retained from the discussion so far is that disinflation was observed during the operation of the EMS, both inside and outside the system. It follows that for the EMS discipline/credibility hypotheses to be valid, evidence must be provided that lower costs were borne by the countries that carried out the disinflationary process within the EMS.

[66]The findings of Artis and Nachane (1990) based on cointegration tests thus contradict their own findings based on the inflation forecast analysis.

[67]The missing observations are for the period March 1986 - April 1987 when Germany observed deflation, and for the months of May and June, 1987, when German inflation was quite low.

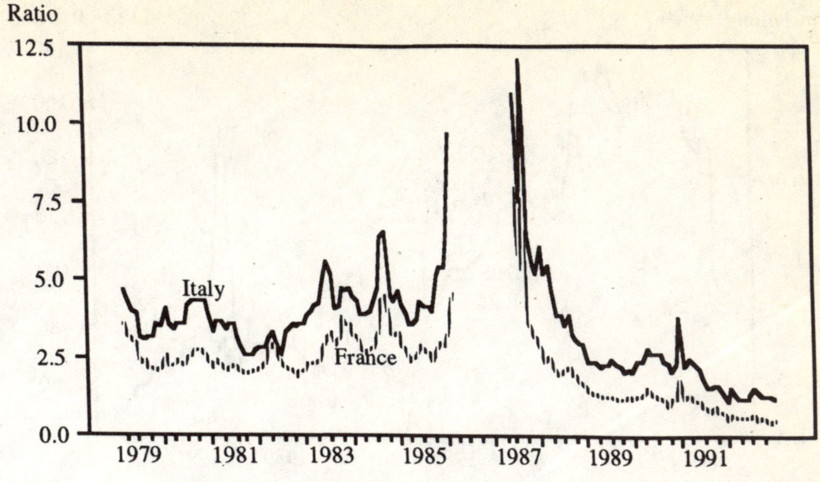

Figure 6.2 - Ratio of French and Italian inflation rates relative to the German inflation rate, 1979-1992
Source: International Financial Statistics (IMF)

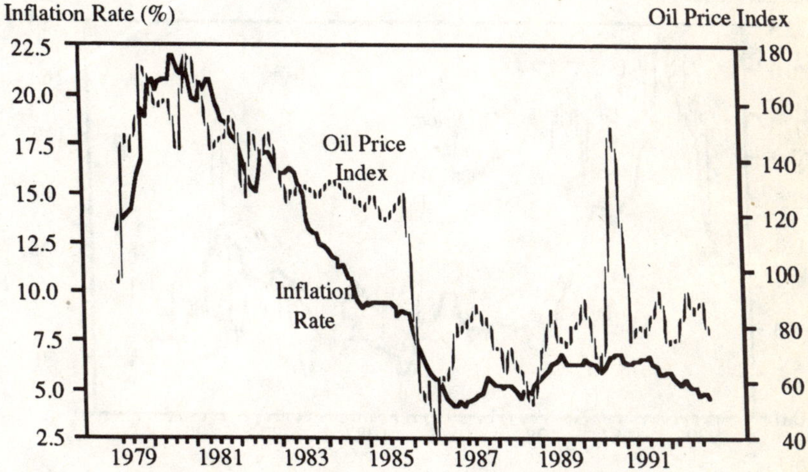

Figure 6.3.a - Italian inflation rates and oil price indeces, 1979-1992
Source: International Financial Statistics (IMF)

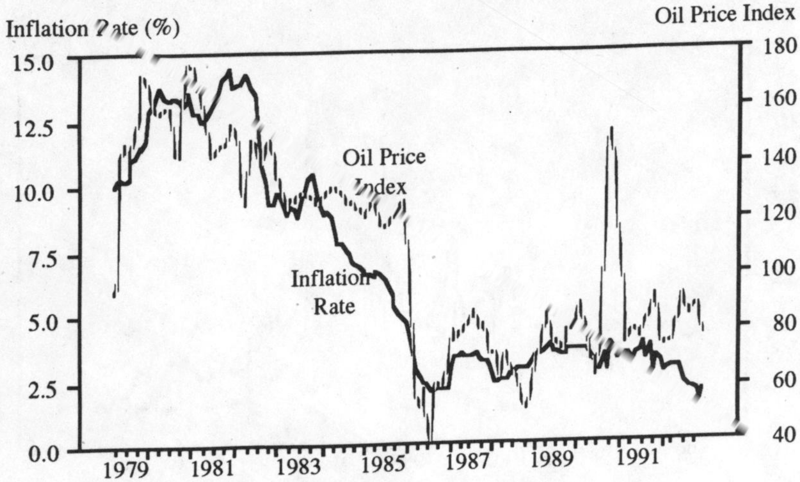

Figure 6.3.b - French inflation rates and oil price indeces, 1979-1992
Source: International Financial Statistics (IMF)

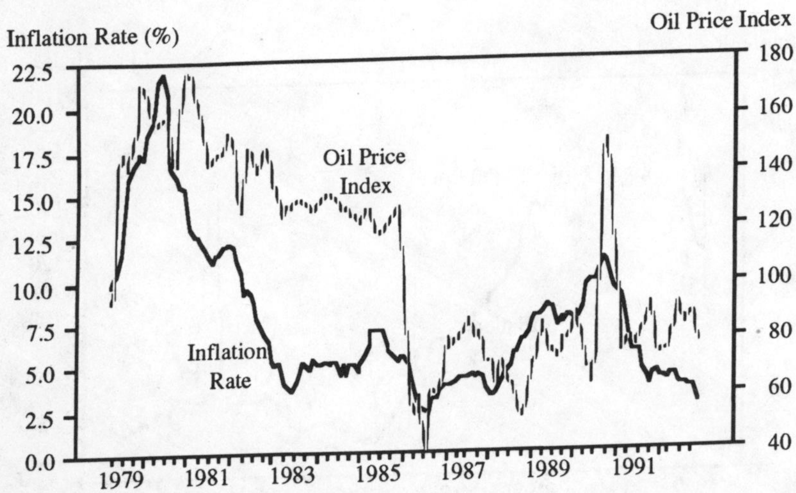

Figure 6.3.c - U.K. inflation rates and oil price indeces, 1979-1992
Source: International Financial Statistics (IMF)

To study the EMS discipline/credibility hypotheses empirically, Giavazzi and Giovannini (1988) apply the "Lucas (1976) critique" using VAR models of price inflation, wage inflation, and output growth. The background is that a shift in policy regime, if clearly identified in time, should be reflected in shifts in the statistical relationships between economic variables. Two types of tests are proposed. In the first approach, the three-variable-VAR model is estimated over a long-time span, covering both a pre-EMS period and an EMS period. The test consists of looking for statistical parameter shifts around the time of the launching of the EMS. Finding a statistical shift would be an indication of the effects of EMS membership. In the second approach, the starting point is the same type of VAR model, but covering only the period preceding the EMS. On the basis of the estimated model, forecasts for the EMS period are computed and compared with the actual figures.

Using German, Danish, French, Italian, and British data, Giavazzi and Giovannini do not find sufficiently robust results to make the EMS credibility hypothesis convincing. In the first approach, the hypothesis of no change in the parameters in the second quarter of 1979 is not statistically rejected in thirteen out of the fifteen equations estimated. The two exceptions are the equations for French inflation. Concerning the second approach, the results are not uniform. Price and wage inflation after 1979 are systematically overpredicted for France and Denmark, while, in the Italian case, they are underpredicted. Output growth is systematically overpredicted for France and underpredicted for Denmark, while no systematic pattern is found for Italy. Summarizing these findings leads to the conclusion that only Denmark benefitted from the credibility that the EMS supposedly gave its members. The results become even more inconclusive when the forecasts obtained for the United Kingdom are taken into account: British inflation rates after 1979 are generally overpredicted, while the output is generally underpredicted. Paradoxically, the EMS discipline/credibility hypotheses would then apply to United Kingdom which, during the period, was not a member of the system. On the whole, Giavazzi and Giovannini's results leave little hope for the validity of the EMS discipline/credibility hypotheses.

6.5. The record of the unemployment/inflation trade-off

The validity of the EMS discipline/credibility hypotheses would ideally be tested by comparing real activity data of the members after 1979 with what would have resulted had they not joined the system but adopted the same anti-inflationary policies. Since only the former type of data is available in practice, we are left with a comparison of EMS countries with non-EMS ones. To identify changes around 1979, we use data from the fall of the Bretton Woods regime onwards.

The bar diagrams below present the record on inflation and unemployment during the period from 1973 to 1992.[68] The set of countries can be divided into

[68] The data sources are Labour Force Statistics (OECD) for unemployment and International Financial Statistics (IMF) for inflation. The frequency of the data is annual.

three separate blocks: members of the EMS (Belgium, Denmark, France, Germany, Ireland, Italy, and the Netherlands); other European countries (Austria, Finland, Norway, Sweden, and the United Kingdom); and non-European countries (Canada, Japan, and the United States). Besides inflation and unemployment rates, the diagrams also contain the misery index as a global measure of economic performance. The index is the sum of the two rates.

Figure 6.4 shows that the behavior of inflation rates in the EMS period is quite standard for the three blocks of countries: an increase during the first two years followed by a generalized disinflation until 1986. The diagrams further show that, for all countries, the price of disinflation was increased unemployment. It is interesting to note that it was in the EMS countries that unemployment increased in a very visible way. In France, increasing unemployment was already visible before 1979. During the EMS period, the rate of unemployment remained persistently high. The EMS was thus not able to slowdown the unemployment trend. The story for Belgium is essentially the same. The only difference is that Belgium had inherited higher rates of unemployment from the "Snake" period and, therefore, the relative increase from one period to the other was smoother. In Germany and the Netherlands, unemployment rates during the worst years of the EMS reached levels twice as high as before the EMS.

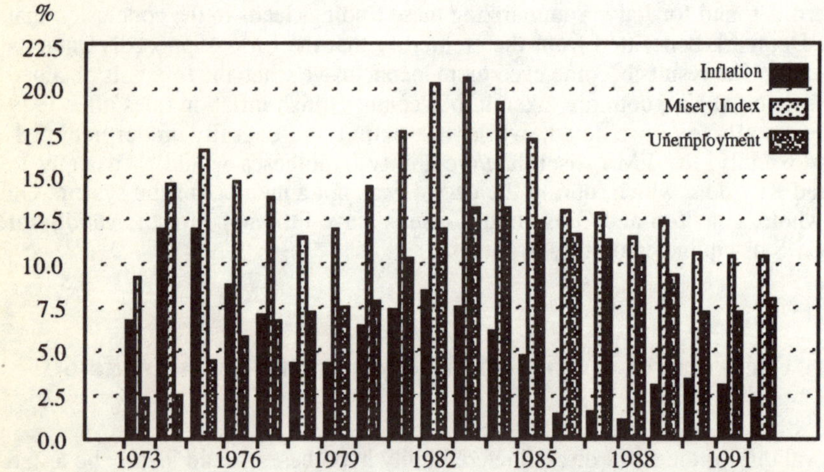

Figure 6.4.a - The unemployment/inflation trade-off in Belgium, 1973-1992

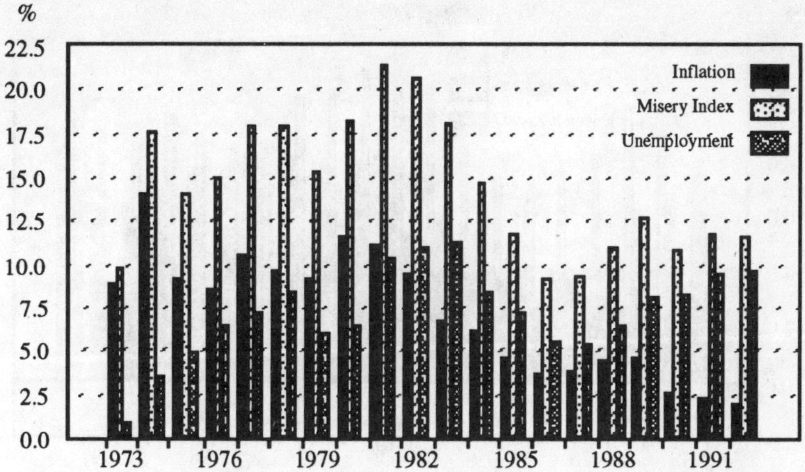

Figure 6.4.b - The unemployment/inflation trade-off in Denmark, 1973-1992

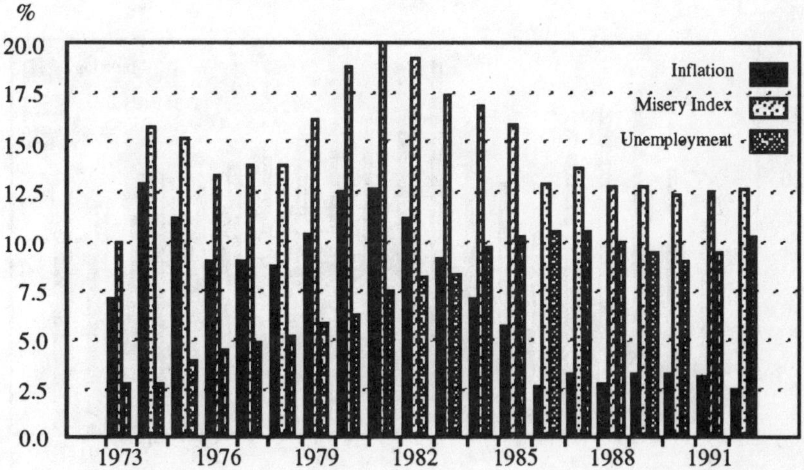

Figure 6.4.c - The unemployment/inflation trade-off in France, 1973-1992

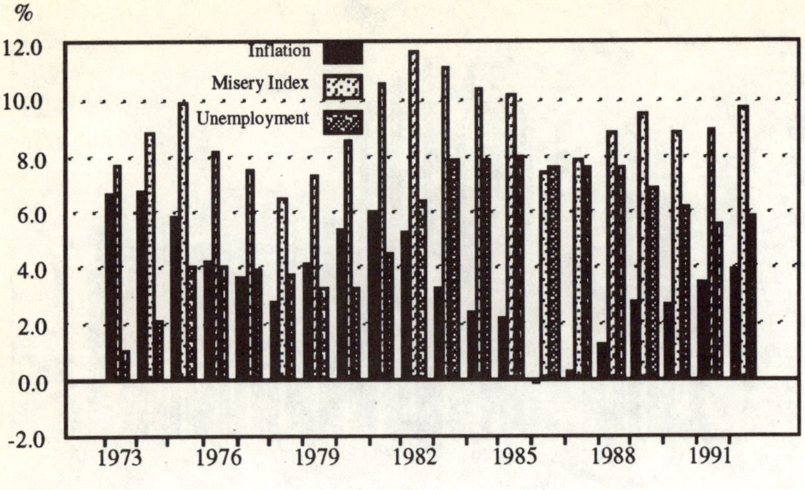

Figure 6.4.d - The unemployment/inflation trade-off in Germany, 1973-1992

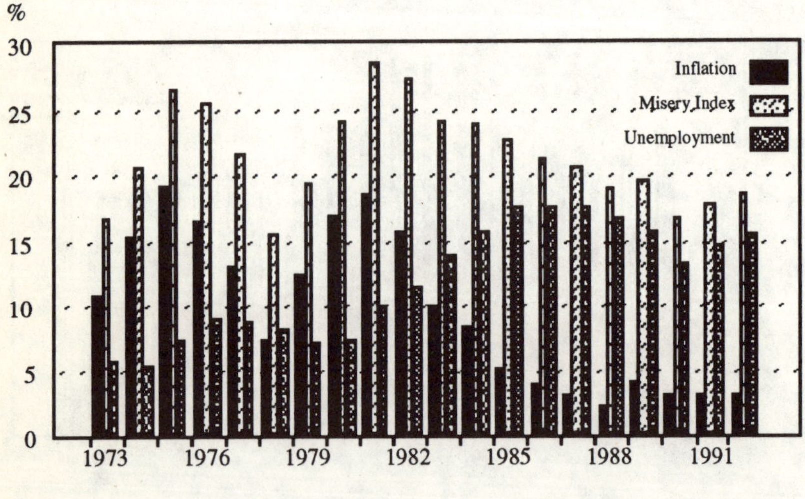

Figure 6.4.e - The unemployment/inflation trade-off in Ireland, 1973-1992

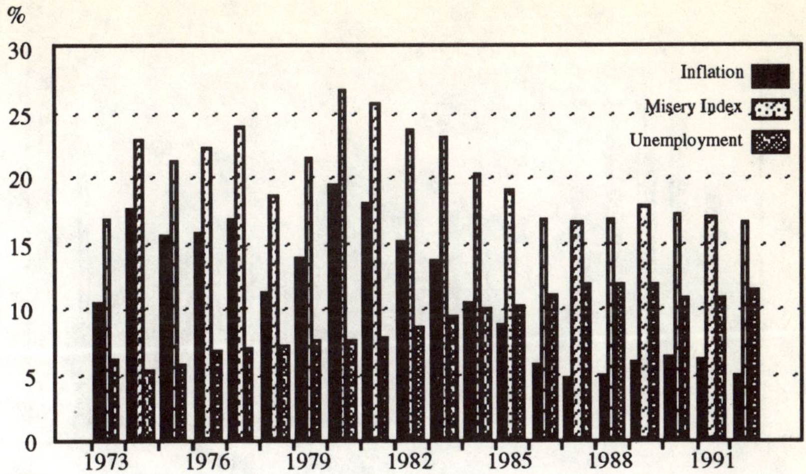

Figure 6.4.f - The unemployment/inflation trade-off in Italy, 1973-1992

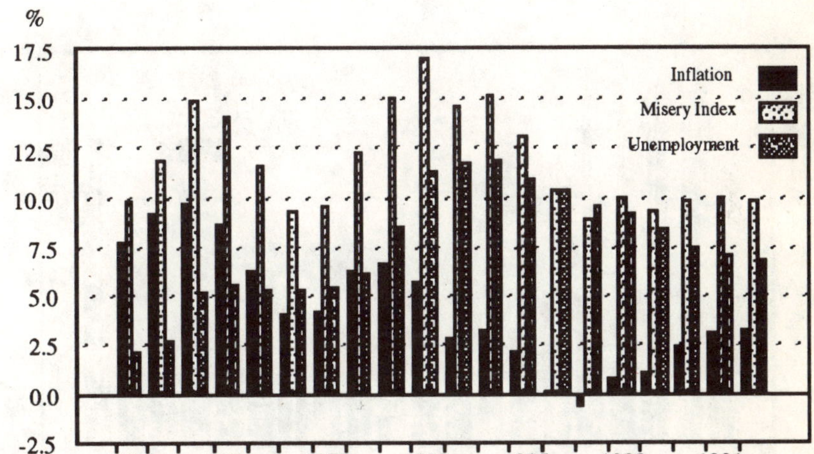

Figure 6.4.g - The unemployment/inflation trade-off in the Netherlands, 1973-1992

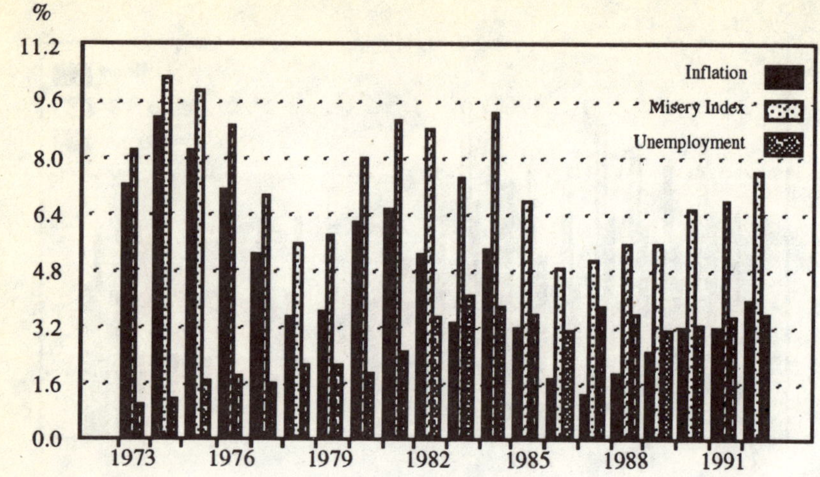

Figure 6.4.h - The unemployment/inflation trade-off in Austria, 1973-1992

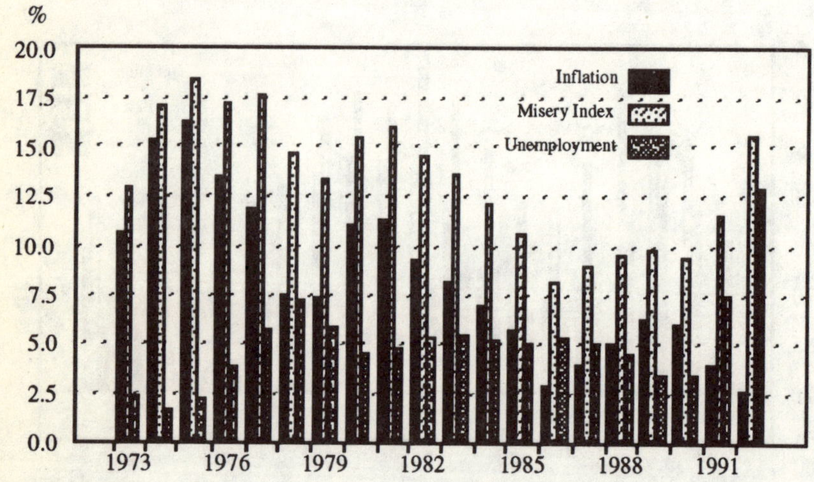

Figure 6.4.i - The unemployment/inflation trade-off in Finland, 1973-1992

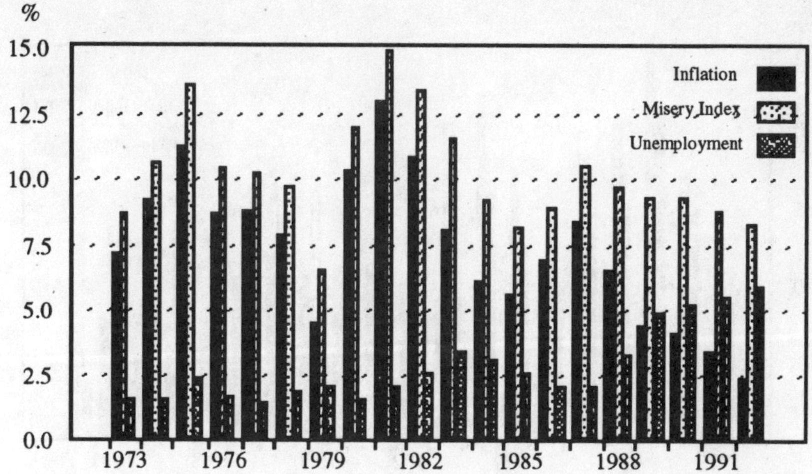

Figure 6.4.j - The unemployment/inflation trade-off in Norway, 1973-1992

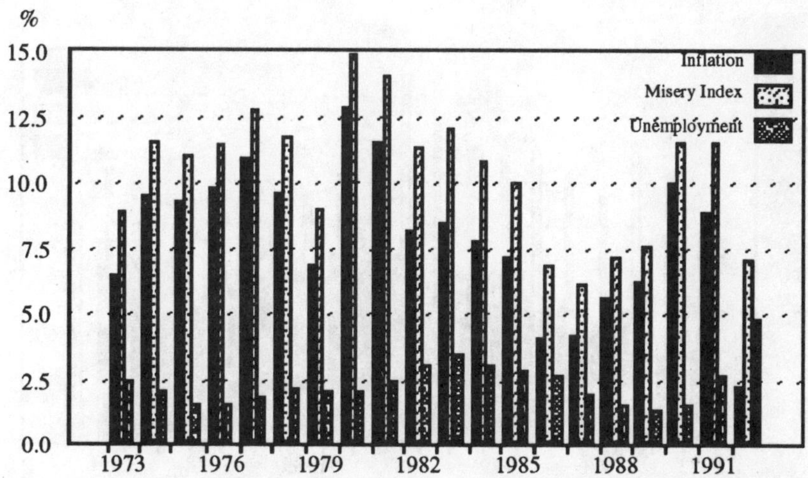

Figure 6.4.k - The unemployment/inflation trade-off in Sweden, 1973-1992

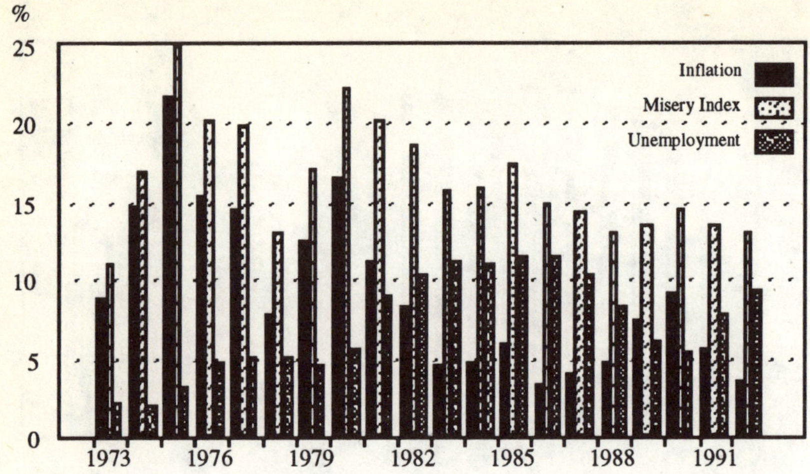

Figure 6.4.l - The unemployment/inflation trade-off in the U.K., 1973-1992

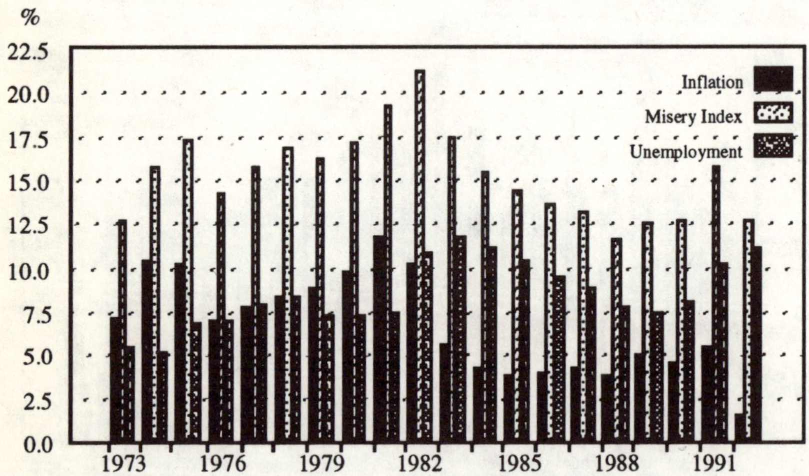

Figure 6.4.m - The unemployment/inflation trade-off in Canada, 1973-1992

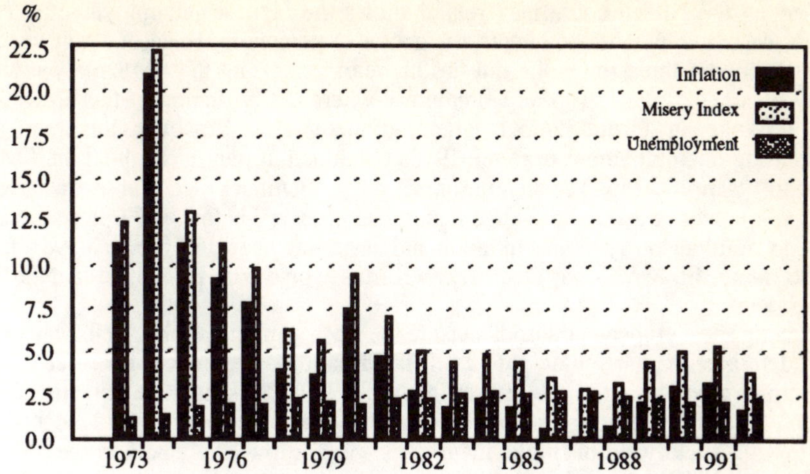

Figure 6.4.n - The unemployment/inflation trade-off in Japan, 1973-1992

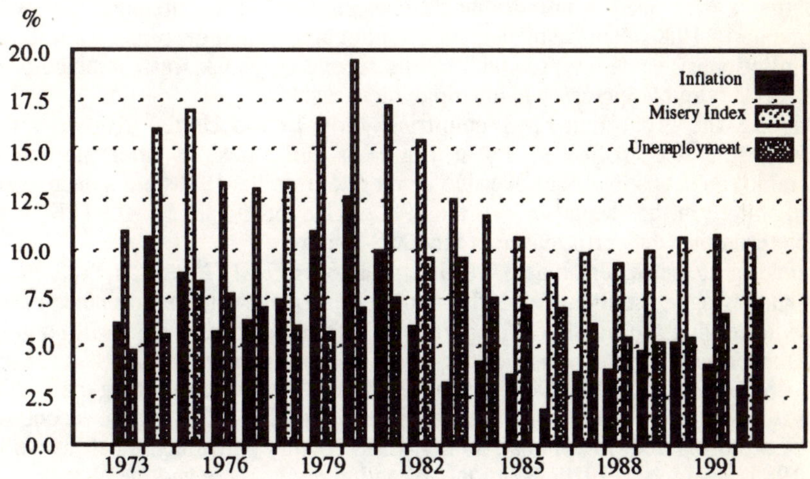

Figure 6.4.o - The unemployment/inflation trade-off in the U.S., 1973-1992

Among the fifteen countries, Ireland shows the highest unemployment rates. Here, we observe unemployment rates above 15 percent in the second half of the 1980s, almost three times the rate in the years preceding the EMS. Italy is the only member of the European Community where the beginning of the EMS did not provoke an abrupt jump in unemployment rates. However, the trend of increasing unemployment from the 1970s continued in Italy throughout the EMS period. Among the EMS members, only Denmark was able to keep unemployment at levels not worse than those observed before 1979. It was even able to simultaneously reduce inflation and unemployment rates between 1983 and 1986. Note, however, that Denmark performs worse than its non-EMS Nordic neighbours.

Among the European countries outside the EMS, Austria, Finland, Norway and Sweden are of particular interest. In Finland, a tendency for increased unemployment was fought off during the 1980s. Austria was able to keep unemployment rates at levels which never exceeded 4 percent in the two decades reviewed. In Norway, unemployment rates were at low levels both in the 1970s and in the 1980s; unemployment rates are, however, slightly higher in the latter than in the former period. Sweden was able to disinflate with rates of unemployment which did not substantially exceed those observed during the 1970s.

Outside Europe, Japan is the country that clearly beat the EMS countries in terms of unemployment performance. The Japanese case is remarkable since inflation was reduced from more than 20 percent in 1974 to extremely low levels by the early 1980s. This achievement did not come with a deep recession. Even the inflationary tendency provoked by the second oil shock was contained with virtually negligible increases in unemployment rates.

Among the eight non-EMS countries, only in the United Kingdom the disinflation was followed by a jump in the rates of unemployment. Unemployment rose twofold over the worst rate from the 1970s but a decreasing trend started in the second half of the 1980s. The performance of the U.K. very much resembles the performance of the EMS countries.

Looking at the misery index, we find peaks in 1974-1975 and in 1980-1983. Not surprisingly, the industrialized economies had their worst performance in the years following the oil shocks. Apart from Denmark, there is no EMS country that performed unambiguously better in the 1980s than in the 1970s. As for the non-EMS countries, Finland and Japan show better performance during the 1980s. This is also true for Sweden and Canada, if the first years following the second oil shock are discarded. In contrast, no non-EMS country performed much worse in the 1980s than in the 1970s. With the exception of Germany and the Netherlands and Denmark in 1986 and 1987, no EMS country reached a misery index below ten percent in the second half of the 1980s. However, levels below ten percent were achieved by Austria, Finland, Norway, Sweden, Japan, and the U.S.. The good performance of Germany and the Netherlands is due to the excellent performance with regard to inflation. At the other extreme, Italy and Ireland are the only countries to reach a misery index above fifteen percent in the second half of the 1980s.

To summarize the comparisons, Table 6.1 contains the average (CPI) inflation rates and growth rates of industrial production (IPI) for the EMS and the non-EMS countries. The mean values are computed with quarterly data over 1975:1-1979:1 and 1983:1-1992:2 and, therefore, exclude the immediate impacts of the oil shocks. As can be seen in the table, there was a significant decrease in average inflation in all countries except Switzerland; this country shows, however, the lowest mean inflation rate in the period before 1979. As for output growth, no country belonging to the EMS shows a significant change in the mean. Two countries outside the EMS (Sweden and Switzerland) were, however, able to achieve an increase in output growth.

Table 6.1 - Mean values of inflation and output growth before and after 1979

EMS	CPI Inflation	IPI Growth
Belgium	7.8*3.5	0.2/2.1
Denmark	9.3*4.2	2.1/3.1
France	9.6*4.4	1.1/1.7
Germany	4.0*2.1	1.2/2.8
Italy	14.7*7.3	1.7/1.6
Netherlands	7.0*1.9	0.1/2.5
Ireland	13.7*4.7	5.1/6.8
Non-EMS		
Unit. Kingd.	14.6*5.4	1.5/1.5
United States	7.1*3.8	3.7/3.2
Canada	8.5*4.4	1.7/2.5
Japan	7.7*1.8	2.5/4.0
Austria	5.9*2.9	1.6/3.3
Norway	8.9*5.7	5.0/4.9
Sweden	9.6*6.7	-2.5*0.7
Switzerland	2.6/3.1	-1.9*2.8

Note: Each cell contains two figures separated by either * or /. The first figure in each cell is the mean value for the period 1975:1-1979:1, while the second one is for the period 1983:1-1992:2. The * was used when the two values are statistically different at the 5 percent level, while in the opposite case they are separated by /.
Source: International Financial Statistics (IMF).

In sum, the members of the EMS did not, in general, perform better after 1979 than other countries. Furthermore, it seems that the unemployment costs of disinflating were higher inside the EMS than outside.[69]

[69]De Grauwe (1987; 1990) gives two explanations for the higher employment costs incurred by EMS countries. One is that these countries followed more restrictive fiscal policies since 1982 than the rest of the industrialized world. The other is that some EMS countries have institutional set-ups which lead to inefficient wage bargaining processes.

6.6. The EMS as a device for self-imposed discipline

Under the EMS, losses of competitiveness due to inflation differentials were never fully recovered in realignments. This is shown in Figures 6.5.a and 6.5.b which depict the cumulative monthly changes in the exchange rates of the Italian lira and of the French franc against the Deutsche mark, and the cumulative monthly inflation differentials between Italy and France against Germany, in the period from March 1973 to December 1992.[70]

The vertical difference between these two lines indicates the cumulative real exchange rate appreciation of the lira and the franc compared to the levels of March 1973 and March 1979, for the pre-EMS and EMS periods, respectively.

For the period beginning in 1979, the concave shape of the cumulative inflation differentials shows that French and Italian inflation had a tendency to converge to the German inflation. If the real exchange rate prevailing at the beginning of the EMS was an equilibrium rate, that equilibrium only prevailed in 1979. From then on, there was persistent overvaluation of the lira and the franc.[71]

The behavior of the LIT/DM and FF/DM real exchange rates between the end of the Bretton Woods regime and the beginning of the EMS was quite different from the record after 1979. As can be seen in the diagrams, in the pre-EMS period the cumulative changes in the nominal LIT/DM exchange rate fell below the line of the cumulative inflation differential only temporarily (between August 1975 and December 1975) and in small amounts. In the period from 1973 to 1979, the FF/DM real exchange rate was overvalued relative to the March 1973 level for about one year. In the remaining five years the behavior of the franc was similar to that of the lira.

The persistent real appreciations of the franc and the lira after 1979 do not reflect the design of the EMS. Instead, it was a self-imposed practice. As noted by Østrup (1992), "*since 1983, EMS countries have by and large gotten their exchange rate wishes fulfilled ... Further, exchange rate adjustment developments since 1983 indicate that external pressure through the EMS has been more effective in making countries devalue rather than the opposite.*" Participating in the EMS and not asking for realignments that fully recover competitiveness might be a strategy adopted by countries with a tradition of high inflation rates. The perverse effects on real exchange rates may prevent countries from promoting inflationary policies. As nicely illustrated by Hughes-Hallett *et al.* (1990), in this strategy we can find "*a parallel with the aversion therapy sometimes used for cigarette smokers where a drug is taken which causes smoking to be accompanied by nausea.*"

The purpose of this section is to test whether by joining the EMS the high-inflation countries lost incentives to create inflation due to self-imposed real exchange rate appreciation.

---

[70]Cumulative inflation differentials are based on consumer price indeces.

[71]According to Vona and Bini-Smaghi (1988), these real exchange rate appreciations would not have been possible in the absence of positive contributions to growth coming from outside the EMS area, namely the real appreciation of the U.S. dollar and other non-ERM currencies and the fast growth of the U.S. economy.

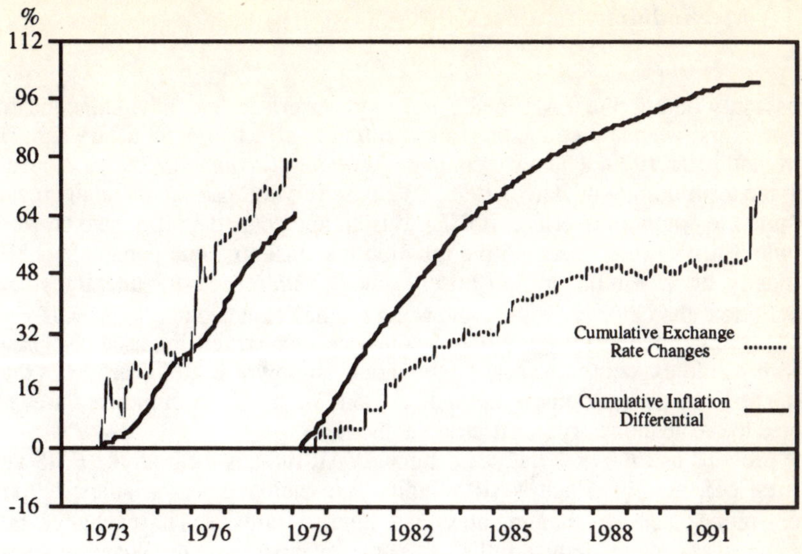

Figure 6.5.a - LIT/DM real exchange rate changes, 1973-1992
Source: International Financial Statistics (IMF)

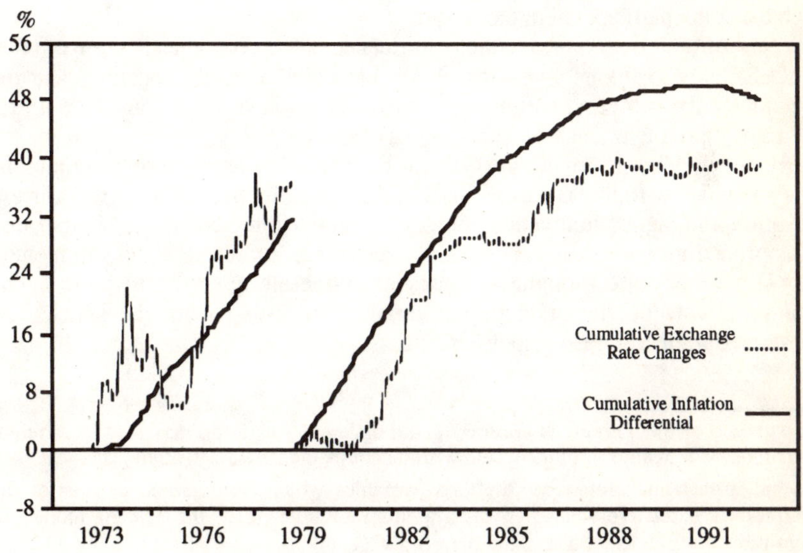

Figure 6.5.b - FF/DM real exchange rate changes, 1973-1992
Source: International Financial Statistics (IMF)

6.6.1. Methodology

To assess whether the EMS made inflation surprises less advantageous for policymakers, we compare the output and inflation effects of a monetary surprise before and after 1979. Thus, we compare "*simulated dynamic Phillips curves*", using the terminology of Barro (1978). We base this comparison on an aggregate measure, the "output net effect" (ONE). It is computed as the difference between the output growth response and the inflation response to a one-percent shock in the money stock. Similar to the "misery index" with respect to unemployment and inflation, the ONE gives the same weight to inflation and output growth.[72]

If, by joining the EMS, high-inflation countries adopted self-imposed discipline, then we would expect that shocks to the money supply lead to lower ONEs than in the pre-EMS period. This would indicate that the monetary authorities are less tempted to create monetary surprises under the EMS.

We proceed as follows. First, we estimate VAR models for both the EMS and the pre-EMS periods. Each VAR contains five endogenous variables: output, prices, money, DM-exchange rates, and interest rates.[73] The exchange rate equations also contain German inflation as an exogenous variable. We allow for an intercept in each of the equations of the VARs. The models for the period beginning in 1979 include dummy variables for the realignment months in which clear breaks in the exchange rate series are observed. In the case of France, dummy variables are also used in the model of the pre-EMS period for the months in which the franc participated in the "snake".[74]

Because of their importance in the performance of the economies, oil prices enter the VARs as exogenous variables.[75] An additional variable considered in the exogenous part of the model are wage rates. As we have seen, wages are a predetermined variable in the theoretical model of section 6.2.

Next, the VARs are inverted to obtain their moving average representations. Each variable is thus expressed as a linear combination of its own current innovation and lagged innovations of all the variables in the system. The purpose of this procedure is to assess the systems' responses to random shocks in money. Shocks in money are thought to represent deliberate government policy. The dynamic effects on the endogenous variables resulting from the shocks are summarized in the impulse response functions.

---

[72]The choice of the weights is arbitrary and a different weighting may lead to different conclusions. The results provided below are accompanied by a sensitivity analysis.

[73]Output, prices and money are the three variables which are common to most of the VAR models extensively used in the literature to investigate the role of money in determining output. See, for example, Sims (1980a,b), Gordon and King (1982), Litterman and Weiss (1985), Bernanke (1986), and Blanchard (1989).

[74]The dummies for the EMS period relate to March 1981, October 1981, and July 1985 for Italy, and October 1981, June 1982, March 1983, and April 1986 for France. The dummies for the French "Snake" periods refer to August 1973 - December 1973 and July 1975 - February 1976.

[75]The contribution of oil shocks to recessions is documented by, for example, Hamilton (1983).

6.6.2. Data

The methodology described above is applied to Italy and France since these are the best examples for the hypothesis of self-imposed discipline in the EMS.[76] The data for the pre-EMS period refer to March 1973 through February 1979. For the EMS period, the data is from March 1979 to December 1988, the period of disinflation where eleven realignments occurred. The set of variables used in the VARs is reported in Appendix 6.A.

All variables are defined in first difference form in order to achieve stationarity. Stationarity was checked through augmented Dickey-Fuller tests[77] (not reported) and plots of the time series as well as their autocorrelation functions.[78]

The number of lags in the VARs is reported in Appendix 6.B. Two aspects were considered in the choice of the lag length. First, it was necessary to preserve enough degrees of freedom in order to make the computation of the impulse responses feasible. The choice of the lag length was thus conditioned by the number of observations available for the shorter period, the pre-EMS one. Second, the residuals should not be autocorrelated. Bearing these two aspects in mind, we followed a two-step procedure. First, we assigned four lags to each variable in each equation. In the second step, and when required, we made small adjustments in the initial number of lags in order to reduce the probability of autocorrelation in the residuals. For that purpose, we applied the m-test proposed by Breusch (1978) and Godfrey (1978), using the five-percent significance level as the decision criterion.

Since the computation of impulse responses does not require the orthogonalization of the residuals across equations, we did not estimate any contemporaneous effects. This assumes that a shock in the money supply in a given period has direct and indirect effects on the endogenous variables in the following periods, but not immediately. This seems quite plausible since we make use of monthly data.[79]

---

[76]Ireland would also be an interesting case study but lack of sufficient data prevents us from carrying out the analysis.

[77]See Dickey and Fuller (1981).

[78]Since we use variables in difference form, the information about any long-run equilibrium relation is lost. Using the two-step procedure suggested by Engle and Granger (1987), we have checked whether two specific long-run relationships held. These are the long-run movement of wages and prices, and the relative version of the PPP theory. The hypothesis of cointegration between wage and price inflation and the relative PPP theory were both rejected. The rejection of constant real prices (and/or wages) can be explained by, for example, productivity gains which are transferred to wages. Given the plots in Figures 6.5.a and 6.5.b, the statistical rejection of the PPP theory is not surprising for the periods and countries investigated.

[79]Our assumption is supported by the fact that the estimated contemporaneous correlations across the residuals are, in general, low.

6.6.3. Results

Figure 6.6.a displays the dynamic responses of the LIT/DM exchange rate to a one-percent shock in the Italian money supply. The corresponding diagram for the FF/DM exchange rate is provided in Figure 6.6.b.[80]

Figure 6.6.a shows that a money supply shock causes the lira to devalue almost three times more in the pre-EMS regime as compared with the EMS.[81] The ultimate devaluations of the lira amount to 0.46 percent and 0.17 percent, respectively. In the case of France, Figure 6.6.b shows that the long-run effects are even more different across the two exchange regimes: the devaluation of the FF/DM in the pre-EMS period is seven times larger than under the EMS period. The ultimate devaluation of the French franc amounts to 0.35 percent and 0.05 percent in the pre-EMS and EMS periods, respectively.[82]

According to the hypothesis of self-imposed discipline in the EMS, the weaker exchange rate devaluation in the period beginning in 1979 would lower the temptation to create money surprises. If this is the case, monetary authorities would have obtained more utility with monetary surprises in the pre-EMS regime than in the EMS, i.e, the ONE measure should have higher values in the pre-EMS than in the EMS period. This part of the hypothesis is also supported by the results. Figure 6.7.a contains the Italian ONE impulse response functions for the two periods, while the ONE impulse response functions for France are provided in Figure 6.7.b.

[80]We have considered a horizon of 48 months since by the end of that time all the dynamic responses had died down. In order to allow for a comparison across countries, we use the same scale for the impulse response functions for each variable. Selected values of the impulse response functions can be found in Appendix 6.C.

[81]As in most applied studies with VAR models, no measure of estimation uncertainty is provided here. The reasons are two. On the one hand, the significance of the estimations is very sensitive to the assumptions that have to be made. The bootstrap method is the technique most commonly used but the quality of the resulting estimations for the standard errors can be questioned [See Lütkephol (1990)]. On the other hand, with the available techniques, the significance bands tend to widen very quickly when impulse responses are cumulative, like ours. This would easily make any response function not significant.

[82]The ultimate effects of money supply shocks in the LIT/DM and FF/DM exchange rates confirm the results of Gros (1989) who found that the variability of EMS exchange rates has been reduced to the minimum achievable with the given variability in the fundamentals. The impulse response functions also show that the swings in the exchange rates are more limited after 1979, compared to the period before 1979. This could be the result of the fluctuation bands of the EMS and is in accordance with previous findings of Rogoff (1985b) and Artis and Taylor (1988), among others, who show that the exchange rate volatility of EMS currencies became lower after 1979.

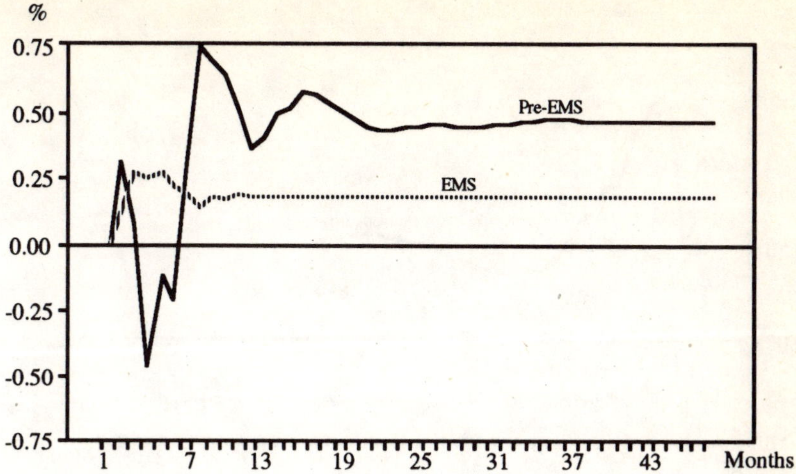

Figure 6.6.a - Cumulative impulse responses of exchange rate changes, Italy

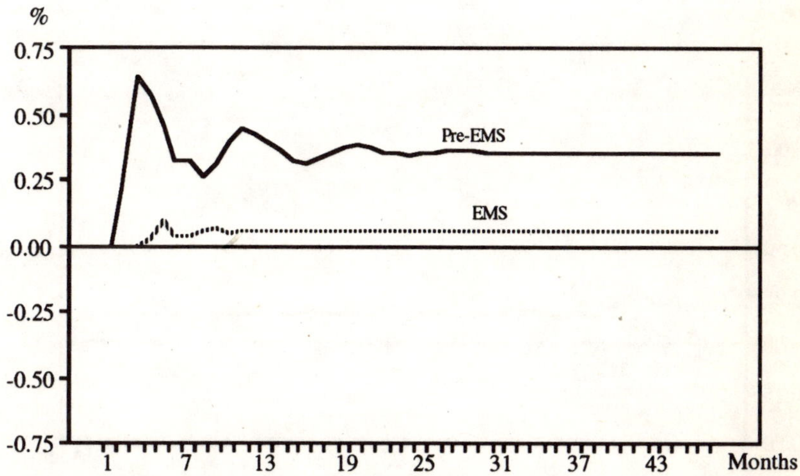

Figure 6.6.b - Cumulative impulse responses of exchange rate changes, France

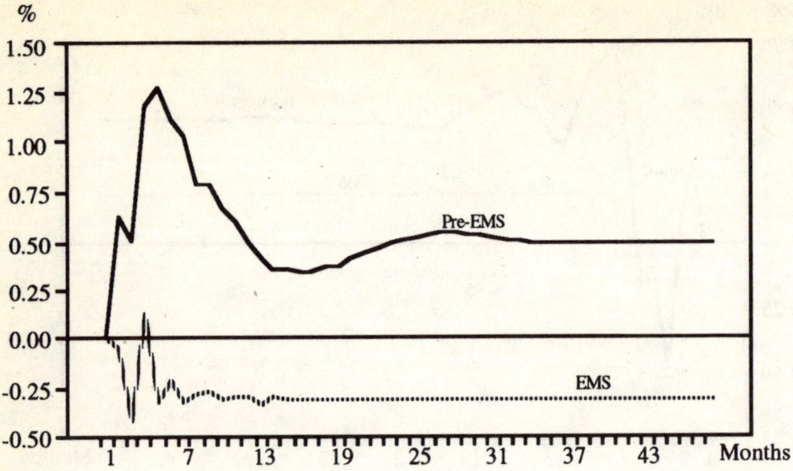

Figure 6.7.a - Output net effect, Italy

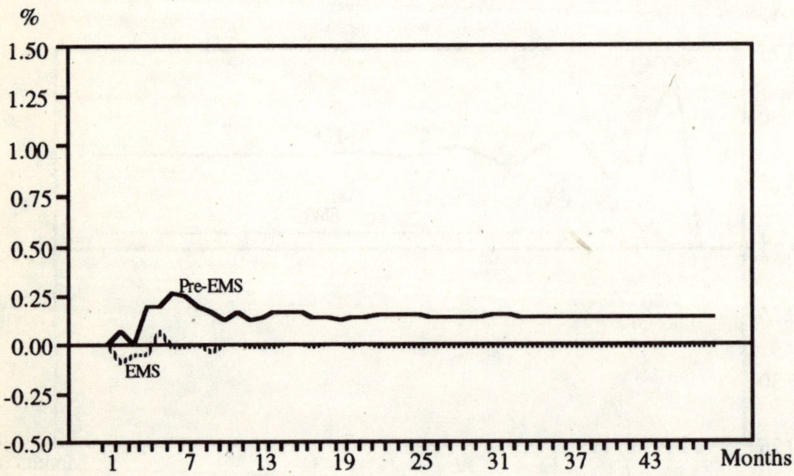

Figure 6.7.b - Output net effect, France

The use of monetary surprises in Italy was more advantageous in the pre-EMS period than in the EMS. Monetary surprises in the EMS even lead to negative values for ONE. In the case of France, Figure 6.7.b shows that the distinction between the two periods is not so clearcut. The ONEs are close to each other and might not be statistically different; even though there is an indication that monetary surprises would have been slightly more tempting in the pre-EMS period than in the EMS. During the EMS period there is no incentive at all for the French monetary authorities to create money surprises, since there is no gain in utility as shown by the fact that the ONE impulse response function and the zero line overlap each other.

Figures 6.7.a and 6.7.b thus show that in the EMS period both the Italian and French monetary authorities had less incentives to create money surprises. The figures also suggest that, before joining the EMS, the monetary authorities in the two countries could achieve some utility by using money surprises.

This conclusion obviously depends on the weights attached to output growth and inflation in the ONEs, which are taken as the global measure of monetary authorities' utility. To see how robust our conclusions are, we compute the weights which would lead to the same long-run values of ONE in both periods and, thus, make the policymakers indifferent about the EMS:

	output growth	**inflation**
Italy	0.08	0.92
France	0.30	0.70

Accordingly, our conclusions would be reversed only if the weight given to output is less than 8 percent and 30 percent for Italy and France, respectively. This does not seem a plausible assumption.

The results thus support the idea of self-imposed discipline: due to higher rigidity of exchange rates, monetary surprises affected output less positively during the EMS period than they did under the previous exchange rate regime.

6.7. Summary and conclusions

The record of inflation rates in EMS countries during the 1980s shows a decreasing and converging trend towards the German levels. This observation gave rise to the "EMS discipline/credibility hypotheses". Given the fact that one of the members of the EMS - Germany - has low inflation rates, the remaining members in the system would adjust their monetary policies towards the German standard. Joining the EMS is thus interpreted as an attempt to borrow the reputation of the Bundesbank. This, in turn, enables the inflation-prone members of the EMS to reduce inflation at a lower cost than would have been the case outside the EMS.

We have noted that the EMS discipline/credibility hypotheses can be questioned both on theoretical and empirical grounds. The EMS is not a system of fixed exchange rates but rather a system of floating rates within a band that can be shifted through realignments. This makes the time-consistent inflation rate in the

EMS similar to the equilibrium rate in a floating-rate system. Furthermore, the hypotheses do not provide an economic explanation for German participation in the EMS and do not explain why is it better to peg the exchange rate than adopt an independent central bank. Concerning the empirical support of the hypotheses, simple data description shows that the decline in inflation in the 1980s was a worldwide phenomenon and that the inflation/unemployment trade-off of EMS countries does not show a better performance than that of non-EMS countries.

The practice of realignments in the EMS in the 1980s was to leave the currencies of high-inflation countries overvalued. This observation suggests that the high-inflation countries adopted real exchange rate appreciation as a strategy to reduce the incentive to inflate. In order to test this hypothesis of self-imposed discipline we investigated whether inflation-prone countries become less tempted to create money surprises after joining the EMS. Our empirical results show that the gain from money surprises decreased in Italy and France with the launching of the EMS. We can, thus, conclude that self-imposed discipline has been a characteristic of monetary policy in the EMS.

Appendix 6.A - Definition of variables and data sources

The data is from the International Financial Statistics of the International Monetary Fund. The variables are defined as follows:

s : Log of spot exchange rate, end of the month. The exchange rate is defined as the number of domestic currency units per DM unit. The DM exchange rates are the result of triangular arbitrage on U.S. dollar exchange rates and are based on *line ae*.

y : Log of output, seasonally adjusted. The industrial production index, seasonally adjusted, (*line 66..c*) is used as the proxy for output.

m : Log of money stock (M1), seasonally adjusted (*line 34..b*).

i : Nominal interest rate (*line 60bs* for France and *line 60b* for Italy).

Δp : Annualized inflation rate. It is computed based on consumer price indeces (CPI), *line 64*. Δp is the CPI log difference between homologous months of two consecutive years.

Δgp : Annualized German inflation rate. Computed in the same way as Δp.

Δw : Annualized wage-inflation rate computed by using wage indeces (WI), *line 65ey* for Italy and *line 65* for France. Δw is the log difference of WI between homologous months of two consecutive years.

oil : Log of (U.S. dollar) crude oil export price index (*line 76aad*).

Throughout the text the Greek symbol Δ is used to denote the first difference of the variables listed above.

Appendix 6.B - Specification of the VAR models

Italy: pre-EMS period

	Δm	ΔΔp	Δs	Δy	Δi	Δoil	ΔΔw	ΔΔgp	m(12)
Δm	1-4	1-4	1-4	1-3	1-4	1-4	1-4	-	0.21
ΔΔp	1-4	1-4	1-4	1-4	1-3	1-4	1-4	-	0.18
Δs	1-4	1-4	1-4	1-4	1-4	-	1-4	1-4	0.73
Δy	1-4	1-4	1-4	1-4	1-4	1-4	1-4	-	0.99
Δi	1-4	1-4	1-4	1-4	1-4	1-4	1-4	-	0.08

Italy: EMS period

	Δm	ΔΔp	Δs	Δy	Δi	Δoil	ΔΔw	ΔΔgp	m(12)
Δm	1-4	1-4	1-4	1-4	1-4	1-4	1-4	-	0.71
ΔΔp	1-4	1-4	1-5	1-4	1-4	1-5	1-4	-	0.07
Δs	1-4	1-4	1-4	1-4	1-4	-	1-4	1-4	0.39
Δy	1-4	1-4	1-4	1-4	1-4	1-4	1-4	-	0.72
Δi	1-4	1-4	1-4	1-4	1-4	1-4	1-4	-	0.61

France: pre-EMS period

	Δm	ΔΔp	Δs	Δy	Δi	Δoil	ΔΔw	ΔΔgp	m(12)
Δm	1-4	1-4	1-4	1-4	1-4	1-4	1-4	-	0.79
ΔΔp	1-4	1-4	1-4	1-4	1-4	1-4	1-4	-	0.92
Δs	1-4	1-4	1-4	1-4	1-4	-	1-4	1-4	0.92
Δy	1-4	1-4	1-4	1-4	1-4	1-4	1-4	-	0.48
Δi	1-4	1-4	1-4	1-4	1-4	1-4	1-4	-	0.88

France: EMS period

	Δm	ΔΔp	Δs	Δy	Δi	Δoil	ΔΔw	ΔΔgp	m(12)
Δm	1-4	1-4	1-4	1-4	1-4	1-4	1-4	-	0.87
ΔΔp	1-4	1-4	1-5	1-4	1-4	1-5	1-4	-	0.05
Δs	1-4	1-4	1-4	1-4	1-4	-	1-4	1-4	0.56
Δy	1-4	1-4	1-4	1-4	1-4	1-4	1-4	-	0.57
Δi	1-4	1-4	1-4	1-4	1-4	1-4	1-4	-	0.33

Notes:

- The (i,j) entry gives the lags of variable j used in the estimation of variable i.
- The column m(12) contains the probabilities of no autocorrelation in the error terms. The allowed maximum order of autocorrelation was set at 12.

Appendix 6.C - Cumulative impulse responses (selected months)

Italy

Months		2	6	12	24	36	48
Δy	Pre-EMS	0.47	1.24	1.01	0.90	0.92	0.92
	EMS	-0.03	0.11	0.05	0.03	0.03	0.03
$\Delta\Delta p$	Pre-EMS	-0.16	0.13	0.52	0.39	0.43	0.42
	EMS	0.02	0.32	0.34	0.34	0.34	0.34
ONE	Pre-EMS	0.63	1.11	0.49	0.51	0.49	0.50
	EMS	-0.05	-0.21	-0.29	-0.31	-0.31	-0.31
Δs	Pre-EMS	0.31	-0.21	0.37	0.44	0.47	0.46
	EMS	0.12	0.21	0.18	0.17	0.17	0.17
Δi	Pre-EMS	0.07	-0.08	0.32	0.19	0.22	0.21
	EMS	-0.03	0.08	0.11	0.11	0.11	0.11
Δm	Pre-EMS	1.21	1.41	1.43	1.37	1.37	1.37
	EMS	1.00	0.87	0.91	0.91	0.91	0.91

France

Months		2	6	12	24	36	48
Δy	Pre-EMS	0.10	0.30	0.19	0.20	0.20	0.20
	EMS	-0.11	-0.07	-0.09	-0.08	-0.08	-0.08
$\Delta\Delta p$	Pre-EMS	0.03	0.04	0.06	0.05	0.05	0.05
	EMS	-0.02	-0.06	-0.08	-0.07	-0.07	-0.07
ONE	Pre-EMS	0.07	0.27	0.13	0.15	0.15	0.15
	EMS	-0.09	-0.01	-0.01	-0.01	-0.01	-0.01
Δs	Pre-EMS	0.21	0.32	0.42	0.34	0.36	0.35
	EMS	-0.01	0.04	0.05	0.05	0.05	0.05
Δi	Pre-EMS	-0.07	0.05	0.06	0.06	0.06	0.06
	EMS	-0.05	-0.09	-0.09	-0.09	-0.09	-0.09
Δm	Pre-EMS	0.69	0.46	0.58	0.54	0.55	0.55
	EMS	0.48	0.48	0.53	0.51	0.51	0.51

CHAPTER 7
In search of a credible EMS

7.1. Introduction

In chapter 5 it was empirically documented that the members of the EMS followed, to different degrees, autonomous monetary policies during most of the 1980s. Autonomy would have been immediately reflected in market exchange rates if these had not been repressed and allowed to move only at discrete realignments. Autonomy combined with fixed exchange rates is, however, unsustainable and requires, sooner or later, adjustments in central parities. This was likely mirrored in the lack of credibility of the fixed exchange rates during the period. It was further shown that, after 1987, the behavior of monetary authorities was changed and the degree of monetary autonomy was quite reduced. In principle, this would imply higher credibility of EMS exchange rate bands, unless shifts in policy were expected.

Our findings are in line with the observation of Giavazzi and Spaventa (1990) who argue that a large improvement in the credibility of the EMS occurred in the second half of the 1980s when a "New EMS" was born. The argument is that exchange controls prior to 1987 enabled the member countries to follow divergent monetary policies which were ratified through realignments in the central parities. The existence of controls on the international movements of capital prevented domestic interest rates from responding to devaluation expectations and, at the same time, shielded central banks' foreign reserves from speculative attacks. In this sense, the dismantling of exchange controls would be compatible only with credibly fixed exchange rates.

Some other views place the improvement of EMS credibility earlier in time. The mere fact that the frequency of realignments decreased after 1983 has been interpreted by some observers as a sign of a more credible EMS.

Gros and Thygesen (1992) put together the two views and assert that "*The credibility of the central rates increases after 1983 (and 1986)*".[83]

The improvement in the credibility of EMS exchange rates has also been officially claimed. The Commission of the European Communities (1991) is very clear in this respect: "*In much of the 1980s, the currencies with the highest interest rates tended to occupy low positions in the ERM band between realignments and to be involved in downward realignments. This reflected a lack of*

[83] See Gros and Thygesen (1992), page 156.

credibility in the ability of the authorities in countries with problems of high inflation and/or worrying budgetary situations to maintain the parity. In a sense, high interest rates were the price that had to be paid by such countries in their attempts, ultimately successful, to establish credibility. More recently, the convergence of inflation among the original narrow-band countries, the absence of realignments over a long period and the momentum of progress towards EMU have gone a long way to convincing markets that EMS realignments are a thing of the past. This has meant that countries with high interest rates have tended to be high in the band, a reversal of the previous pattern. Moreover, these countries have not wanted to decrease their interest rates, because of their anti-inflationary goal."[84]

By the time all these arguments were raised, the last realignment had occurred in January 1987. The EMS was, thus, observing a long period of exchange rate stability. However, the turbulences in the EMS that led to the suspension of sterling and the Italian lira from the ERM, in September 1992, and the widening of the bands, in August 1993, to 30 percent cast doubts on these claims.

This chapter assesses the credibility of the EMS and whether any visible shift in credibility can be found throughout the history of the system. This will allow us to judge whether recent events in the EMS came as a surprise or could have been anticipated.[85] The analysis focuses on the credibility of the DM exchange rates and, therefore, tells us whether German monetary policy provided a credible anchor for the remaining countries of the EMS.

The chapter is organised as follows. In section 7.2, we present a general picture of the credibility of the DM exchange rates, using a test suggested by Svensson (1991a). Empirical evidence presented in the section clearly shows that the test is appropriate to detect a lack of credibility but is not designed to assess statistical shifts. In section 7.3, a method for detecting shifts in the credibility of pegged exchange rates is proposed and implemented. Finally, we provide a summary and conclusions in section 7.4.

7.2. Svensson's "simplest test of target zone credibility"

A straightforward, non-parametric method to provide an overview of the credibility of an exchange rate band was suggested by Svensson (1991a). The test assumes international capital mobility and consists of a comparison of the domestic interest rate with the rate of return implicit in the exchange rate band. When the exchange rate is strictly fixed and credible and capital is sufficiently mobile, agents are indifferent between investments in domestic currency or foreign currency since the domestic and the foreign interest rates are exactly the same for the same maturity. However, this is not necessarily the case when the exchange rate is allowed to float within some margins around a central parity. Let i_t, i_t^*, S_t, S^U, and S^L be the

[84]See Commission of the European Communities (1991), page 208.

[85]Rose and Svensson (1994) found that private-sector agents and policymakers were taken by surprise by the events of September 1992. These conclusions are, however, questioned by Branson (1994) and Tabellini (1994).

domestic interest rate, the foreign interest rate, the exchange rate (defined as the number of domestic currency units per unit of foreign currency), and the upper and lower limits of fluctuation of the exchange rate band, respectively. Assume that the interest rates are of a one-year term. If the central rate is credible, then the domestic interest rate does not necessarily equal the foreign one but is restricted to lie inside a band whose upper and lower limits are, respectively,

$$i^U = \left(1 + i_t^*\right)\frac{S^U}{S_t} - 1 \qquad (7.1.a)$$

and

$$i^L = \left(1 + i_t^*\right)\frac{S^L}{S_t} - 1 \qquad (7.1.b)$$

Assume now that $i_t > i^U$. This can only be a situation in which the exchange rate band is not credible. For if the bands are deemed credible, a safe profit opportunity is available and everyone would borrow abroad and lend at home. This would not be compatible with equilibrium in the international capital market. Thus, it must be the case that when the domestic interest rate is above i^U, a devaluation before maturity is expected. Analogously, $i_t < i^L$ holds only if an appreciation of the domestic currency is expected before maturity.

An alternative approach consists of examining the expected exchange rate. A credible band requires the expected exchange rate, $E_t(S_{t+n})$, to lie inside the allowed margins of fluctuation. That is,

$$S^L \leq E\left(S_{t+n}\right) \leq S^U \qquad (7.2)$$

Assuming that the forward exchange rate, say F_t^{t+n}, is a good proxy for the expected future spot rate, credibility of the exchange rate band requires the forward rate to fall between S^L and S^U. For example, a situation in which $F_t^{t+n} > S^U$ is only compatible with a non-credible band. For, if the target zone is considered credible, everybody would sell foreign currency forward and obtain a safe profit amounting to, at least, $F_t^{t+n} - S^U$ per unit transacted. But then the equilibrium in the forward market would not be possible: everyone would be willing to sell foreign currency forward but nobody would buy such contracts because foreign currency could be purchased later on in the spot market at a maximum price of S^U. A devaluation before the end of period t+n must, therefore, be perceived. Analogously, when F_t^{t+n} is below S^L, an appreciation of the domestic currency before the maturity of the contract must be expected for the forward market to be in equilibrium.

In this type of test, the term of the contracts must be sufficiently long for the results to be minimally reliable. Tests based, for example, on a one-year term are more conclusive than those based on one-week or one-month terms. For if the exchange rate is not credible, the probability of devaluation within the coming year is greater than the probability that the devaluation will occur in the coming week. It follows that if short-term forward rates fall inside the bands, the test is not conclusive and the exchange rate may or may not be credible.

7.2.1. Data

The tests presented below refer to expected exchange rates defined as the number of units of each currency per unit of DM. Expected exchange rates 12 months ahead, $E_t(S_{t+12})$, were computed assuming uncovered interest parity

$$E_t\left(S_{t+12}\right) = S_t \frac{\left(1 + i_t\right)}{\left(1 + i_t^*\right)} \tag{7.3}$$

where i_t^* is the 12-month Euro-mark interest rate and i_t is the 12-month Euro interest rate for each of the remaining EMS currencies.[86,87] The use of the offshore interest rates is recommended because of the existence of capital controls in most of the EMS countries for most of the life of the system.

The data are monthly and based on the last trading day of a month. The test for the Irish punt (IP) covers the period from November 1981 to April 1990. For the remaining exchange rates the samples start in March 1979 and end in December 1992. Since Italy left the ERM in September 1992, the Italian lira is analyzed only until August 1992.[88]

7.2.2. Results

Figures 7.1.a-7.1.f provide the results from the simplest test of exchange rate credibility. Each diagram contains three series: the upper and lower limits of the exchange rate bands and the expected exchange rates. The three series are measured as percentage deviations from the central parities prevailing at the end of the month. Accordingly, the limits of the bands are, throughout the samples, straight lines of ±2.25 percent, except in the case of the LIT/DM exchange rate. The margins of fluctuation for the lira were ±6 percent from the beginning of the EMS and were narrowed to ±2.25 percent in January 1990.

---

[86] As mentioned above, shorter term expectations might lead to inconclusive results. For DM exchange rate credibility tests using 2-days and 1-month expectations, see Flood, Rose, and Mathieson (1990).

[87] If covered interest arbitrage applies, the computed expectations are actually 12-month forward exchange rates. For tests similar to ours but where survey data for expectations are used, see Frankel and Phillips (1991)

[88] All the data until April 1990 are from a database created by Andrew Rose from BIS daily data; I thank Lars Svensson for providing me with the samples. The source for the remaining observations is Financial Times.

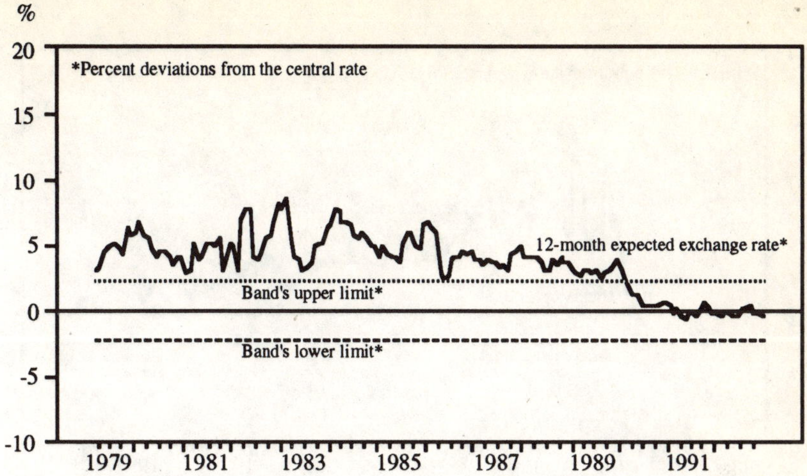

Figure 7.1.a - Credibility of the Belgian exchange rate peg, 1979-1992

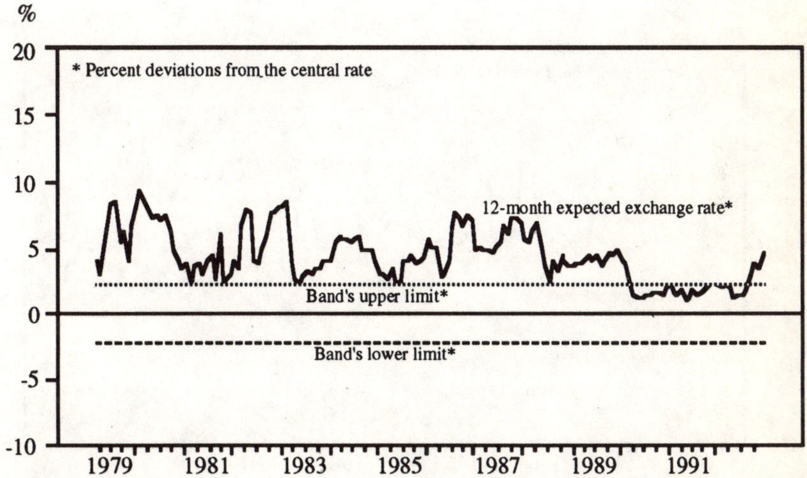

Figure 7.1.b - Credibility of the Danish exchange rate peg, 1979-1992

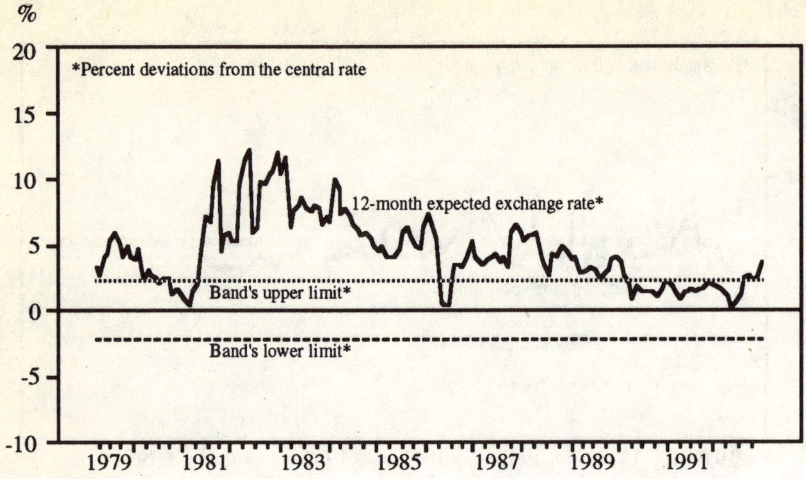

Figure 7.1.c - Credibility of the French exchange rate peg, 1979-1992

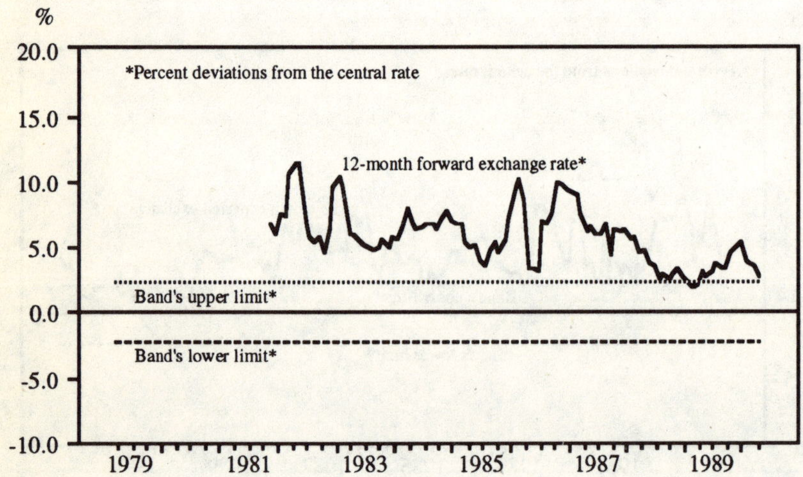

Figure 7.1.d - Credibility of the Irish exchange rate peg, 1981-1990

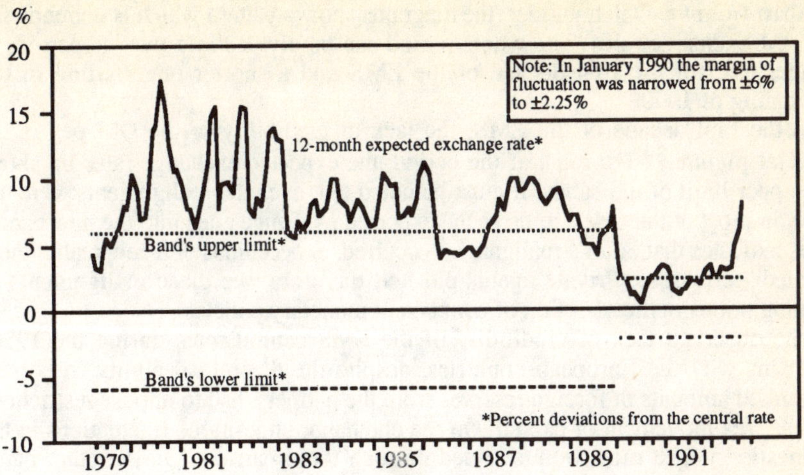

Figure 7.1.e - Credibility of the Italian exchange rate peg, 1979-1992

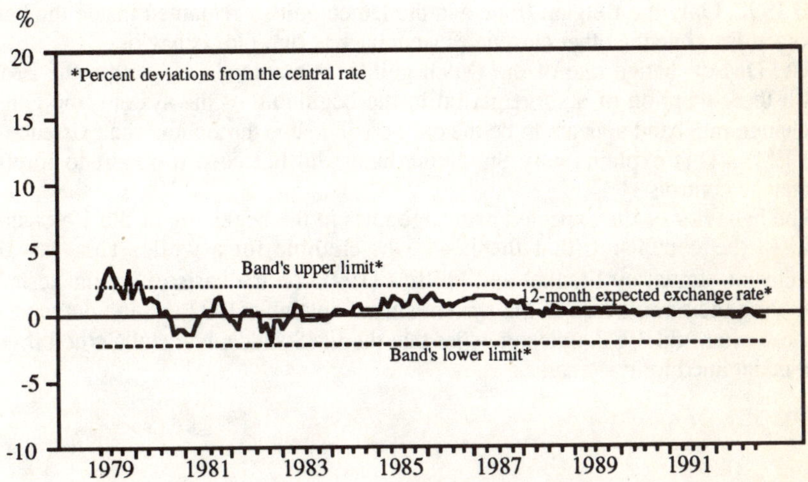

Figure 7.1.f - Credibility of the Dutch exchange rate peg, 1979-1992

Apart from the Dutch guilder, the diagrams show a pattern which is common for all DM exchange rates. The whole period can be divided into two subperiods, a longer one for the first decade of the EMS and a shorter one starting in the beginning of 1990.

In the first decade of the EMS, the lack of credibility of the DM peg is the general picture.[89] For most of the period, the expected exchange rates lie above the upper limit of the bands. It must be noted that even the realignments were not able, in most of the cases, to drive the expected exchange rates into the new bands. This indicates that, after a realignment occurred, expectations of a new realignment immediately arose. Private agents did not, therefore, see those realignments as turning points in the direction of convergent monetary policies.

The observed lack of credibility of the EMS central rates during the 1980s explains why the European countries, despite the theoretical ability to borrow unlimited amounts of foreign reserves from the partners, had to impose restrictions on the free movement of capital. On the one hand, undesirable fluctuations in the domestic interest rates were avoided through these barriers. On the other hand, speculative attacks were dampened. With divergent monetary policies followed by EMS countries, such speculative attacks explained by exchange rate fundamentals would have been frequent since private agents know that countries cannot indefinitely bear persistent losses of competitiveness.[90]

In the beginning of 1990, we can observe a general tendency for expected exchange rates to fall inside the fluctuation limits. This situation continued until mid 1992. Only the Belgian franc and the Dutch guilder remained inside the band afterwards, while the other currencies went back to the "old" behavior.

The DM exchange rate of the Dutch guilder is a unique case within the EMS. With the exception of a short period in the beginning of the system, the Dutch exchange rate band appears to be the only credible one throughout the existence of the EMS. This explains why the Netherlands did not need to resort to foreign exchange controls.

The behavior of the expected exchange rates in the beginning of the 1990s may lead to the conclusion that the EMS was credible for a while. This was the conclusion drawn by Frankel and Phillips (1991) on the basis of similar tests.[91] Knowing the turbulances of the system since September 1992 and the outcome of our test after mid-1992, one concludes that the EMS suddenly lost the credibility it had maintained for two years.

---

[89]This lack of credibility is the most likely explanation for the inability to fit EMS data to the non-linear models of exchange rate determination suggested by Krugman (1991) for target zones. See Flood, Rose, and Mathieson (1990).

[90]Since there are various ways of circumventing capital controls, speculative attacks have been dampened but not fully avoided. For example, the March 1983 realignment of the French franc is often given as an example of a typical result of a balance-of-payments crisis with a final attack. See Penati and Pennacchi (1989) and Agénor, Bhandari, and Flood (1991).

[91]See, also, Frankel *et al.* (1993).

7.3. Improvement of EMS exchange rate credibility

7.3.1. Credibility and forward market excess returns

Throughout the history of the EMS, overprediction of future spot rates by forward rates is a feature common to most of the Deutsche mark exchange rates. This can be seen from Figures 7.2.a-7.2.f which plot monthly forward excess returns for the six exchange markets analyzed in the previous section. Forward excess returns are defined as the logarithmic difference between the three-months-ahead spot rates and the current three-month forward rates (one-month for the Irish punt), and are scaled in order to obtain annualized percentages. Both forward and spot rates are defined as the number of units of each currency per unit of DM. Disregarding some outliers, the diagrams clearly show that, for most of the period, forward excess returns contain a persistent negative component (with the possible exception of the HFL/DM exchange rate).

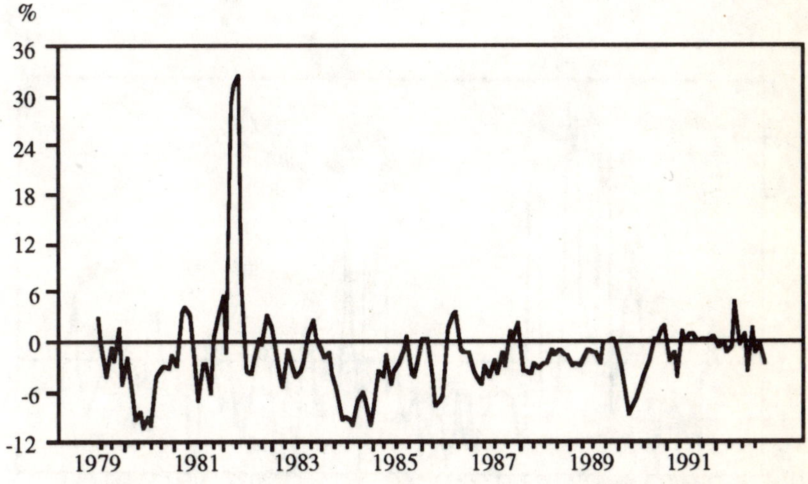

Figure 7.2.a - Forward excess returns on the Belgian franc, 1979-1992

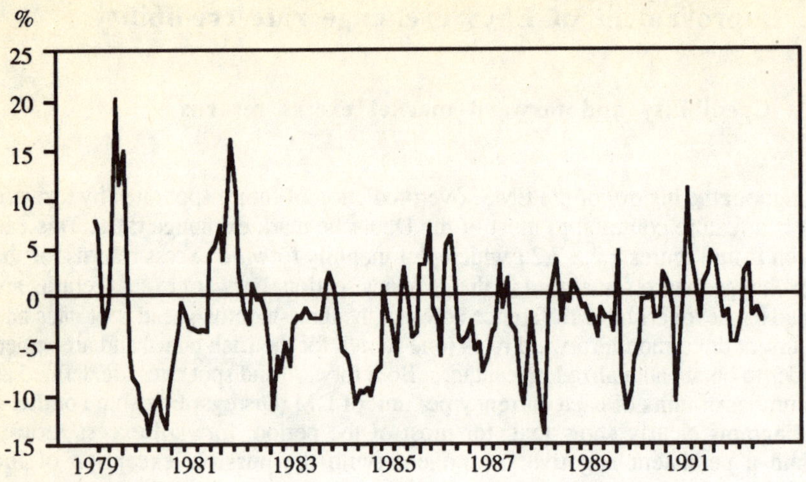

Figure 7.2.b - Forward excess returns on the Danish krone, 1979-1992

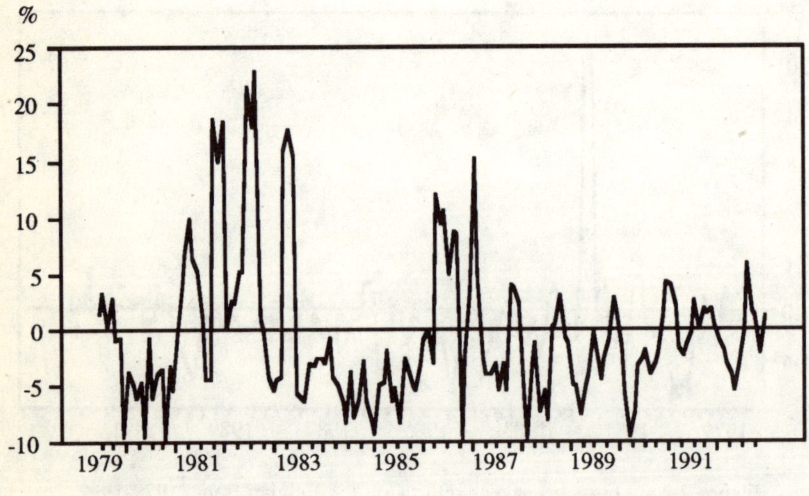

Figure 7.2.c - Forward excess returns on the French franc, 1979-1992

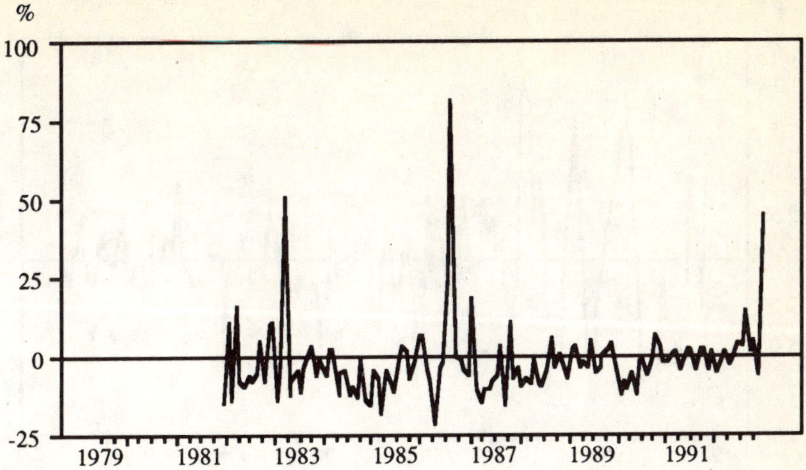

Figure 7.2.d - Forward excess returns on the Irish punt, 1979-1992

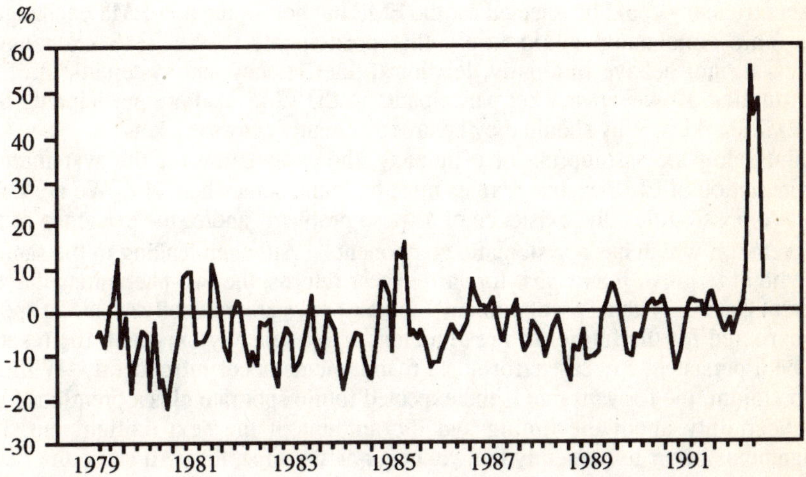

Figure 7.2.e - Forward excess returns on the Italian lira, 1979-1992

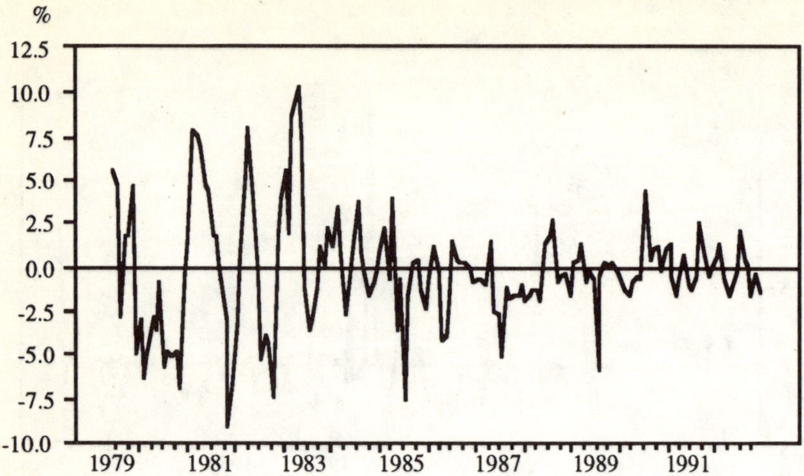

Figure 7.2.f - Forward excess returns on the Dutch guilder, 1979-1992

One explanation for this is given by Jung and Wieland (1990) who analyze the efficiency of EMS and non-EMS DM exchange markets. Their conclusion is that market efficiency could be rejected for the EMS but not for the non-EMS exchange rates. This conclusion would imply that participants in the EMS exchange markets do not behave rationally, leading to inefficiency and systematic profit opportunities. However, market participants in the EMS also are participants in non-EMS markets. Why should they behave differently across markets?

Maintaining the assumption of efficiency, the explanation for the systematic overprediction of EMS exchange rates must be found somewhere else. We are left with two possibilities: the existence of a "peso problem" and/or the existence of a risk premium which has a systematic component.[92] Although leading to the same outcome in terms of the *ex post* forward excess returns, the two phenomena have different causes. With a "peso problem", forward rates are rationally set at the spot rate expected for the future. If a realignment is permanently expected, the result will be a persistent forecast error since realignments occur infrequently. With a risk premium, the forward rate is the expected future spot rate plus a premium for the uncertainty about the timing and the amount of the next realignment. If realignments occur infrequently but can occur at any time, this will cause the risk

[92]The "peso problem" phenomenon is increasingly becoming a popular explanation for the rejection of the unbiasedness hypothesis. The existence of a "peso problem" is used, for example, by Borensztein (1987), Lewis (1989), and Kaminsky and Peruga (1991) to explain the fact that foreign exchange market participants have systematically underpredicted the strength of the U.S. dollar in the first half of the 1980s.

Krasker (1980), for foreign exchange markets, and Lizondo (1983), for foreign exchange futures markets, have shown that conventional efficiency tests are not valid in the presence of "peso problems" and their inappropriate use can result in misleading conclusions.

premium to have a systematic component which is transferred, in turn, to the *ex post* forward excess returns.

The difference between the future spot and the forward exchange rates can thus be interpreted as a forecast error, a realignment risk premium or a combination of both. Regardless of the label, detection of statistically significant systematic excess returns from forward transactions is evidence of a lack of credibility of fixed exchange rates.[93] If the credibility of EMS bands improved with time, one would expect the systematic component of the excess returns to gradually move towards zero.[94] In order to detect shifts which might have occurred in the credibility of EMS exchange rates we are, therefore, going to focus on the behavior of the systematic component of the forward excess returns.

7.3.2. Methodology

The annualized m-month forward excess return, e_t^{t+m}, is defined as:

$$e_t^{t+m} \equiv \left(s_{t+m} - f_t^{t+m}\right)\frac{12}{m}\,100\ , \qquad (7.4)$$

where s_{t+m} is the logarithm of the spot exchange rate in month t+m and f_t^{t+m} is the logarithm of the forward exchange rate contracted at month t to be delivered in m months time.

The various components of the m-month forward excess return can be described by the following expression:

$$e_t^{t+m} = k + \sum_{i=1}^{m-1} \theta_i\, a_{t-i} + \sum_{j=1}^{r} \omega_j\, g_{t,j}\left(\text{Realig}\right) + a_t \qquad (7.5)$$

The first term on the right-hand side of (7.5), k, is a constant. The non-systematic component is given by a_t. In the case of efficient markets, where participants behave rationally, a_t is a white noise process. The second term is a moving average process of order m-1 followed by the m-month forecast errors of overlapping forward contracts [Hansen and Hodrick (1980)]. The third term contains a set of "intervention functions" aimed at assessing the impact of realignments on the forecast errors. These functions are defined as

---

93 A similar explanation is given by Evans and Lewis (1993) to the trends in excess returns that they found in a number of markets.

94 The movement of the systematic excess return towards zero may either be a smooth process [if there is learning as in Lewis (1989)] or take the form of a jump. This would be the case if the "New EMS" applies: dismantling of exchange controls would have suddenly made systematic forecast errors vanish.

$$g_{t,j}(\text{Realig}) = \begin{cases} 1 & \text{if} \quad n \leq t \leq n+m-1 \\ 0 & \text{otherwise} \end{cases} \tag{7.6}$$

where n is the month at which realignment j takes place.

The coefficients of the intervention functions indicate whether the timing and the amount of the change in the central parity was expected by market participants.

Since a non-expected realignment can lead to a maximum of m forecast errors, we should have *r times m* coefficients rather than the r included in expression (7.5). Given the definition of the intervention functions, ω_j represents the average of the m *ex-post* forecast errors resulting from realignment j. Since this average may hide situations in which a realignment in period t is not predicted in month t-m but is predicted, for example, in month t-1, we adopt the following procedure in order to single out whether and when a given realignment was expected. We start by considering ω_j in each intervention function to be a common factor to the m possible forecast errors. When ω_j, under this assumption, is not statistically significant, we make ω_j common only to the first t-m-1 forecast errors. When still not statistically significant, we continue with a similar procedure until ω_j is related only to the earliest forecast error. This procedure assumes that the further away the realignment is, the greater is the possibility of making wrong predictions.

The strategy adopted for detecting improvements in EMS credibility is based on the estimation of k from equation (7.5) and can be divided into three steps. First, we estimate equation (7.5) over the whole sample period. The main purpose is to single out whether the realignments that the EMS underwent were expected by the market. At the same time, we obtain the average of the systematic component of the *ex-post* excess return for the whole period. Second, we use the March 1983 and January 1987 realignments to divide the samples into three periods. This allows us to compare the coefficient k across subperiods of exchange regimes which are supposed to be different. This comparison assumes that in the beginning of each period exchange market operators lose their memory.[95] Third, we compute (7.5) in a recursive manner in order to find out whether and when an increase in EMS credibility occurred, a conventional method for analysing parameter stability [see Hendry (1989)]. In this step, the first estimation covers the first three years for which data is available. One observation is then added to the previous data set, until the last observation is also covered. In contrast to the second step, the recursive estimations assume that exchange market operators have long memories.

[95] Although not with our explicit purpose, step two for the first two sub-periods (1979:3-1983:3 and 1983:3-1987:1) has been performed by Fratianni and von Hagen (1990b) who also decomposed the forward excess returns into the mean and unanticipated realignments. The procedure adopted by Fratianni and von Hagen is essentially the same adopted in this section except that, instead of using a single intervention function for each period, we assign an intervention function to each realignment. Instead of computing the mean of the unexpected realignments during a given time period, our procedure, thus, allows for the computation of the specific unexpected exchange rate change for each realignment.

7.3.3. Data

The systematic component of the forward excess returns is more likely to be found in long- rather than in short-term contracts. There is, however, a drawback in using contracts with a very long term when there are high frequency observations: the order of the moving average becomes high, necessitating the estimation of many parameters. This reduces the degrees of freedom. We resolve this trade-off by using three-month forward rates for the BF/DM, DK/DM, FF/DM, LIT/DM, and HFL/DM and one-month forward rates for the IP/DM. Forward excess returns data are annualized.[96]

Since the Italian lira started floating in September 1992, the assessment of credibility for fixed LIT/DM exchange rates only makes sense until August 1992. For uniformity, the analysis for the remaining DM rates is also conducted until August 1992, allowing us to draw conclusions about how credible they were when the recent strains in the EMS started. The sample starts in June 1979 for all exchange rates except for the Irish punt where the sample starts in December 1981.

7.3.4. Results

Descriptive statistics for the forward excess returns are given in the upper part of Table 7.1. The sample means are negative in all markets, despite the existence of some positive outliers which, as we will show below, are the result of unexpected realignments. Generally speaking, the forward exchange rates have, thus, overpredicted the future spot rates.

The results from the estimation of equation (7.5) over the whole sample are given in the middle part of Table 7.1. Following the estimation procedure described above, only unexpected realignments were considered in the final estimations.[97]

[96]The data for the excess returns of BF/DM, DK/DM, FF/DM, LIT/DM and HFL/DM exchange rates is from the International Financial Statistics (IMF) and Financial Times. For the IP/DM the data comes partly from the same source as in section 7.2 and partly from Financial Times.

[97]The unexpected realignments are those listed in Table 7.1. For comparison, see the list of all EMS realignments in Table 2.1.

Table 7.1 - The forward excess return: Descriptive statistics and estimates[1)]

Descriptive statistics of the forward excess returns[2)]

	BF/DM	DK/DM	FF/DM	IP/DM	LIT/DM	HFL/DM
Period	79:6-92:8	79:6-92:8	79:6-92:8	81:12-92:8	79:6-92:8	79:6-92:8
Sample mean	-1.59**	-2.08**	-0.65	-2.10*	-4.36**	-0.21
	(0.45)	(0.46)	(0.52)	(1.01)	(0.55)	(0.25)
Sample std. dev.	5.66	5.85	6.54	11.47	6.95	3.20
Skewness[3)]	3.51**	0.67**	1.51**	3.96**	0.28	0.37
Excess kurt.[3)]	19.34**	1.44**	2.41**	25.00**	0.11	1.22**
Min. value	-10.43	-13.89	-9.78	-21.66	-21.86	-8.98
Max. value	32.70	20.13	23.00	82.05	15.83	10.29

Estimation of the m-month forward excess return

$$e_t^{t+m} = k + \sum_{i=1}^{m-1} \theta_i a_{t-i} + \sum_{j=1}^{r} \omega_j g_{t,j}(\text{Realig}) + a_t$$

	BF/DM	DK/DM	FF/DM	IP/DM	LIT/DM	HFL/DM
Period	79:6-92:8	79:6-92:8	79:6-92:8	81:12-92:8	79:6-92:8	79:6-92:8
No. of observ.	159	159	159	129	159	159
Deg. of freedom	154	152	151	123	151	154
k	-2.13**	-2.59**	-1.92**	-3.43**	-5.38**	-0.36
	(0.43)	(0.65)	(0.61)	(0.59)	(0.81)	(0.39)
θ_1	0.67**	0.81**	0.77**		0.74**	0.67**
	(0.07)	(0.07)	(0.06)		(0.06)	(0.07)
θ_2	0.56**	0.56**	0.70**		0.62**	0.51**
	(0.07)	(0.07)	(0.06)		(0.06)	(0.07)
$\omega_{79:9\text{-}79:11}$		7.14*			12.37**	6.33**
		(3.12)			(3.92)	(2.00)
$\omega_{79:11\text{-}80:1}$		16.05**				
		(3.09)				
$\omega_{81:3\text{-}81:5}$					11.54**	
					(3.90)	
$\omega_{81:10\text{-}81:11}$					10.50**	
					(2.90)	
$\omega_{81:10\text{-}81:12}$	6.82**	7.99*	20.0**			
	(2.15)	(3.05)	(2.89)			
$\omega_{82:2\text{-}82:4}$	29.18**	8.40**				
	(2.13)	(3.07)				
$\omega_{82:6\text{-}82:8}$			20.2**			
			(2.90)			
$\omega_{83:3}$				53.83**		
				(6.56)		
$\omega_{83:3\text{-}83:5}$			19.0**			8.08**
			(2.87)			(1.98)
$\omega_{85:7\text{-}85:9}$					20.93**	
					(3.88)	

(Continued in next page)

(Table 7.1 - Continued from the previous page)

	BF/DM	DK/DM	FF/DM	IP/DM	LIT/DM	HFL/DM
$\omega_{86:4}$				-18.23**		
				(6.56)		
$\omega_{86:4-86:6}$			15.3**			
			(2.88)			
$\omega_{86:8}$				85.47**		
				(6.56)		
$\omega_{87:1}$			4.96*	21.94**	6.84*	
			(2.14)	(6.56)	(3.03)	
Corrected R^2	0.81	0.65	0.77	0.68	0.61	0.49
Q[4)]	(36) 34.5	(36) 36.1	(36) 44.7	(33) 29.8	(36) 35.7	(36) 49.3

Descriptive statistics of the estimated non-systematic forecast errors

	BF/DM	DK/DM	FF/DM	IP/DM	LIT/DM	HFL/DM
Period	79:6-92:8	79:6-92:8	79:6-92:8	81:12-92:8	79:6-92:8	79:6-92:8
Sample mean	-0.06	-0.09	-0.05	0.00	0.04	-0.06
	(0.19)	(0.27)	(0.24)	(0.56)	(0.33)	(0.18)
Sample std. dev.	2.40	3.38	3.05	6.41	4.22	2.25
Skewness[3)]	0.02	0.25	-0.12	0.38	-0.23	-0.05
Excess kurt.[3)]	0.57	1.00*	1.27**	0.35	0.27	1.22**
Min. value	-6.80	-11.24	-11.37	-14.73	-14.05	-6.48
Max. value	6.43	10.49	9.21	19.21	10.77	7.06

1) Forward excess returns are measured in annualized percentage rates.

2) 3-month forward excess returns (except for Ireland where the forward returns are on 1-month basis).

3) The Skewness and Excess kurtosis statistics are used for testing normality. Normality would require them to be statistically equal to zero.

4) Ljung-Box Q-statistic for autocorrelation of the residuals. Q follows approximately a chi-square distribution with the number of degrees of freedom equal to the selected number of lags. The number of lags used in the test precedes, within parentheses, the computed statistic.

Note: ** and * denote rejection of non-statistical significance on the 1% and 5% levels of significance, respectively. The figures in parentheses, below the regression coefficients, are the standard errors.

Despite the lack of credibility of the BF, DK, FF, IP, and LIT during most of the EMS period, as well as for the HFL in the beginning of the system, our results show that some realignments were unexpected or underpredicted. The underprediction is reflected by the positive signs of all ωs. The only exception is $\omega_{86:4}$ for the IP/DM exchange rate, which is negative and statistically significant. This coefficient indicates that market participants were expecting a realignment in the IP/DM exchange rate to occur in April 1986. In fact, in April 1986 there was a realignment, but not of the Irish punt. The expectations were, however, not unjustified as shown by the eight percent devaluation of the IP/DM exchange rate, a few months later, in August 1986. By then, the market participants were fully surprised, as reflected by the $\omega_{86:8}$ coefficient of 85.47 percent (since the data is annualized, this figure represents a forecast error of 7.1 percent).

The results reported in the middle part of Table 7.1 also show three cases in which realignments that were not expected three months in advance, became anticipated before maturity. This can be seen in the subscripts of the ωs. For the Italian lira, the October 1981 realignment was anticipated by September, while the January 1987 realignment was anticipated two months in advance, i.e., by November 1986. The January 1987 realignment was also anticipated in the FF/DM exchange market two months in advance.[98]

As required by an efficient market, the non-systematic component of the computed forecast errors (net of the forecast errors resulting from unexpected realignments) are not serially correlated. This can be seen from the relatively low figures of the Ljung-Box Q-statistic.[99] Further descriptive statistics of these errors are provided in the lower part of Table 7.1.[100]

Apart from the HFL/DM exchange rate, the estimation of equation (7.5) over the whole sample period shows that the systematic component of the excess returns is significantly negative, meaning that market participants systematically and significantly overpredicted the future spot rates. A remarkably large value of -5.4 percent was estimated for the LIT/DM exchange rate. The remaining estimates are -3.4, -2.6, -2.1 and -1.9 for the Irish punt, Danish krone, Belgian franc and French franc, respectively.[101] The HFL/DM is the only exchange rate for which the average excess return is not statistically significant. These results confirm the impressions from the previous section.

The estimation of equation (7.5) for each of the sub-periods defined above leads to the estimates of the intercept k reported in Table 7.2.

---

[98]The method implemented in this section is appropriate to assess, *ex post*, whether or not the level and/or the timing of a realignment is expected. For the *ex ante* assessment of the probability and size of devaluations, different methods can be found in the literature, particularly in the context of the Balance-of-Payments crises literature. Most of these models have been implemented with Latin-American data. See, for example, Blanco and Garber (1986) and Goldberg (1990) who have dealt with the Mexican peso, and Cumby and van Wijnbergen (1989) who have analyzed the Argentinian peso. Recently, Rose and Svensson (1991), Svensson (1991b), and Frankel and Phillips (1991) have estimated expectations of future realignments of the EMS exchange rates, based on a model of market's expectations suggested by Bertola and Svensson (1990).

[99]The only exception is the HFL/DM forecast errors which pass the test with a small margin. Fratianni and von Hagen (1990b) found a autoregressive process of order one in weekly HFL/DM forecast errors data.

[100]According to the skewness and excess kurtosis tests for normality reported in the bottom of Table 7.1, we find two data series of forecast errors failing the 5 percent criterium. We were able to overcome this problem by using dummy variables for non-realignment related observations where some outliers seem to emerge. The relevant results were, however, not changed.

[101]The data used in section 7.2 are forward exchange rates if covered interest parity applies. If the systematic component of the excess return is interpreted as a systematic risk premium, the lines representing the expected exchange rate in Figures 7.1.a-7.1.f should be moved downwards, meaning a less negative picture for the credibility of EMS exchange rates. The same reasoning applies for the measure used by Rogoff (1985b) for assessing EMS exchange rate volatility. (For the specific period analyzed by Rogoff, the persistent excess returns are provided below.)

Table 7.2 - Systematic forward excess returns in different sub-periods, 1979-1992

Sub-periods	BF/DM	DK/DM	FF/DM	IP/DM	LIT/DM	HFL/DM
Until 1983:3	-1.93	-3.18*	-0.84	-2.66	-7.83**	-0.23
	(1.00)	(1.33)	(1.08)	(2.67)	(1.69)	(1.12)
1983:3-1986:12	-3.02**	-2.65**	-3.48**	-5.01**	-7.43**	-0.41
	(0.80)	(0.72)	(0.99)	(0.89)	(1.40)	(0.67)
After 1986:12	-1.63**	-2.38*	-2.10**	-2.61**	-2.81**	-0.37
	(0.47)	(1.00)	(0.74)	(0.71)	(1.06)	(0.28)

Note: ** and * denote rejection of non-statistical significance on the 1% and 5% levels of significance, respectively. The figures in parentheses, below the regression coefficients, are the standard errors.

The following can be noted from Table 7.2. In each of the sub-periods, the intercept is non-significant for the guilder, suggesting that the HFL/DM rate has been permanently credible. The first row in the table also shows that, in the beginning of the EMS, only the Italian lira and the Danish krona were not credible. In the second sub-period, the intercepts became significantly negative, suggesting that credibility deteriorated. In the most recent sub-period, represented by the last row, all DM exchange rates except the guilder continued to lack credibility. The point estimates in the third sub-period are, however, lower than in the second.

To assess whether exchange rate credibility improved, we added a dummy variable to equation (7.5) to check the stability of the intercept across the three sub-periods. As repoted in Table 7.3, for none of the estimations was the dummy statistically significant at the one percent level. In the case of the lira, and at lower levels of significance, there might be some statistical improvement in the credibility of the DM band after the January 1987 realignment.

The stability of the systematic *ex-post* forward excess return across the operation of the EMS is convincingly confirmed when equation (7.5) is estimated in the recursive manner previously described. The recursive estimates of the systematic component of the forward excess returns are plotted in Figures 7.3.a-7.3.f together with ±2 standard errors of the estimates.[102,103]

[102] The fact that as information accrues the estimates precision improves is reflected in the fall of the standard errors of the estimates. This is an expected statistical result.

[103] The coefficients are plotted against the last observation of each of the recursively increasing samples. According to the data sets used in this study, the first estimation covers the period 1981:12-1984:11 for the IP/DM and should have covered the period 1979:6-1982:5 for the remaining exchange rates. However, due to non-convergence for smaller data sets of the Gauss-Newton algorithm used in the estimations, the first estimation for the DK/DM excess returns covers the period 1979:6-1983:5.

Table 7.3 - The March 1983 and January 1987 realigments and the stability of systematic forward excess returns

	BF/DM	DK/DM	FF/DM	IP/DM	LIT/DM	HFL/DM
Estimation period	79:6-86:12	79:6-86:12	79:6-86:12	81:12-86:12	79:6-86:12	79:6-86:12
Dummy=1	83:6-86:12	83:6-86:12	83:6-86:12	83:4-86:12	83:6-86:12	83:6-86:12
k	-1.85*	-3.42**	-1.01	-2.66	-7.39**	-0.19
	(0.88)	(1.17)	(1.15)	(1.87)	(1.49)	(0.90)
Δk	-1.44	1.04	-2.24	-2.36	0.50	-0.14
	(1.24)	(1.62)	(1.62)	(2.17)	(2.10)	(1.25)
Estimation period	79:6-92:8	79:6-92:8	79:6-92:8	81:12-92:8	79:6-92:8	79:6-92:8
Dummy=1	87:4-92:8	87:4-92:8	87:4-92:8	87:2-92:8	87:4-92:8	87:4-92:8
k	-2.57**	-2.79**	-1.96*	-4.39**	-6.84**	-0.43
	(0.54)	(0.84)	(0.78)	(0.86)	(1.02)	(0.51)
Δk	1.06	0.48	0.09	1.79	3.53*	0.15
	(0.83)	(1.26)	(1.19)	(1.17)	(1.55)	(0.78)

Note: ** and * denote rejection of non-statistical significance on the 1 percent and 5 percent levels of significance, respectively. The figures in parentheses, below the regression coefficients, are the standard errors.

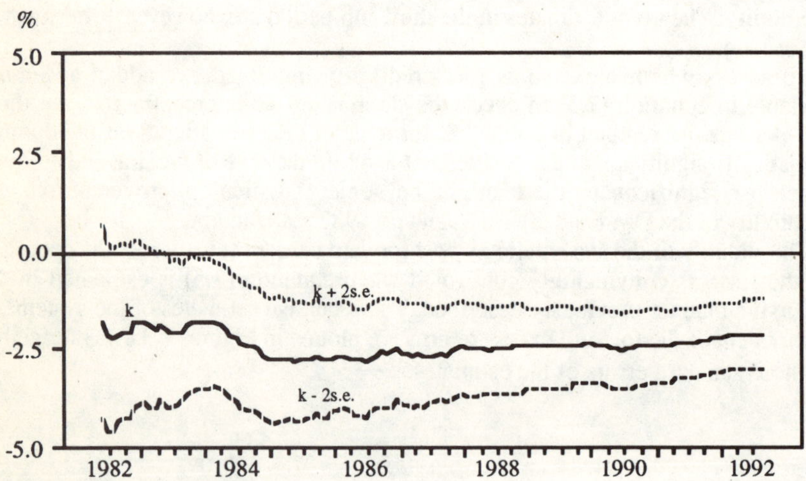

Figure 7.3.a - Recursive estimates of BF/DM systematic forward excess returns

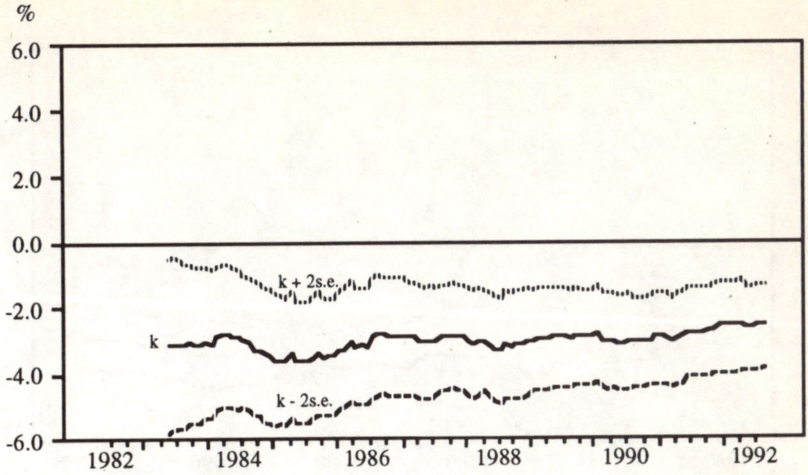

Figure 7.3.b - Recursive estimates of DK/DM systematic forward excess returns

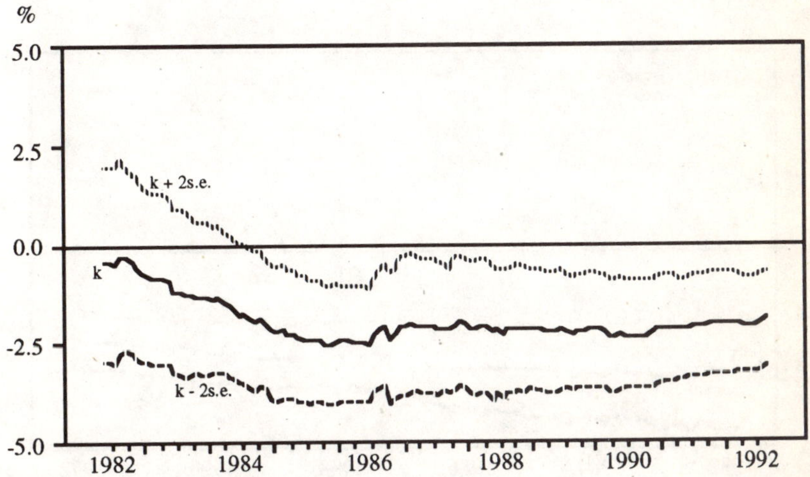

Figure 7.3.c - Recursive estimates of FF/DM systematic forward excess returns

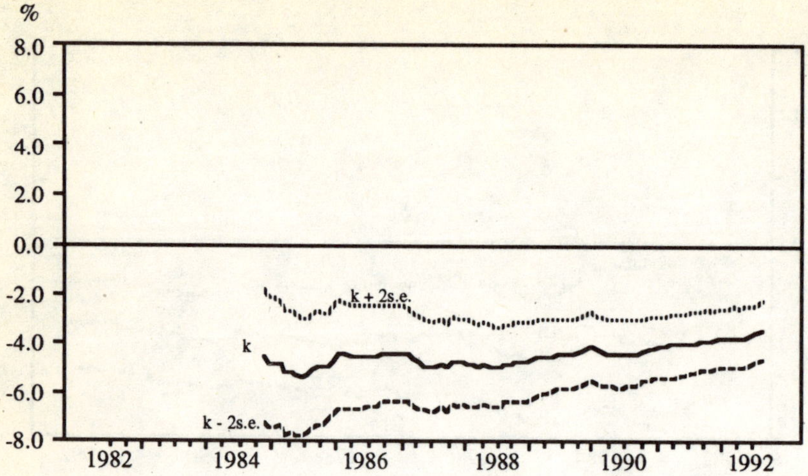

Figure 7.3.d - Recursive estimates of IP/DM systematic forward excess returns

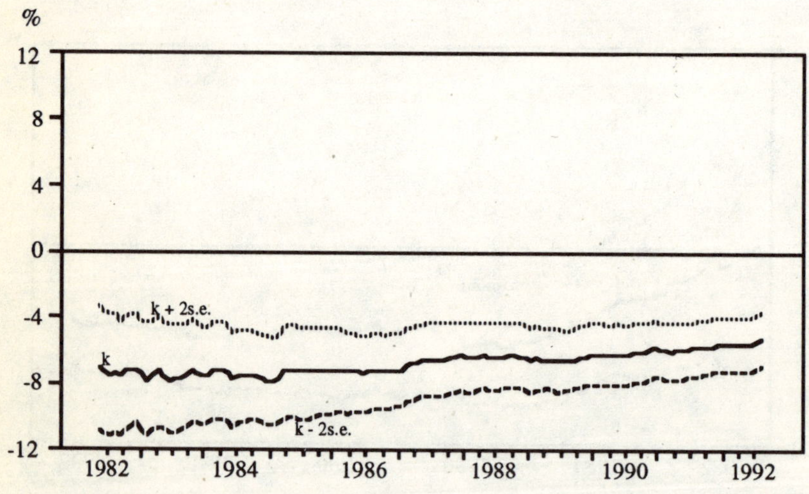

Figure 7.3.e - Recursive estimates of LIT/DM systematic forward excess returns

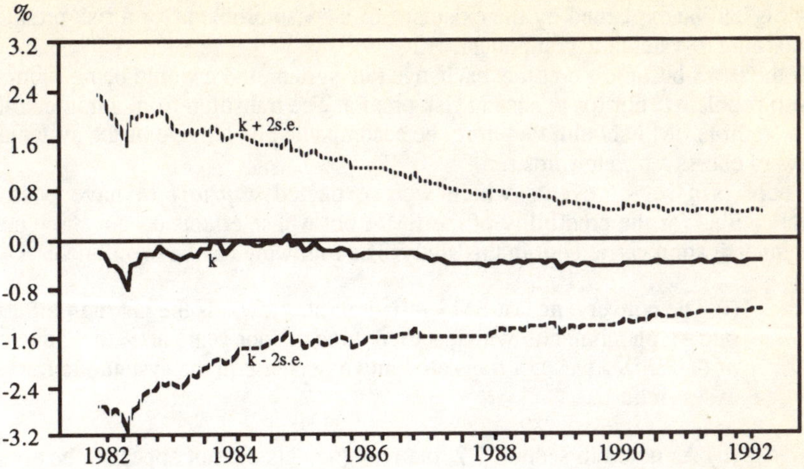

Figure 7.3.f - Recursive estimates of HFL/DM systematic forward excess returns

The main conclusion from these diagrams is that parameter stability cannot be rejected. This suggests that the alleged improvement in the credibility of the EMS was not statistically visible during the period under investigation. At no point in time did the persistent excess returns move significantly towards zero. In the particular case of the FF/DM the opposite occurred, i.e., the systematic component of the forward excess return falls to statistically negative values when the sample period is extended beyond the middle of 1984.

7.4. Summary and conclusions

Svensson's test of target zone credibility shows a non-credible EMS for most of the existence of the system. The only exception is the guilder/mark exchange rate. Disregarding short-lived episodes, the expected exchange rates lie above the upper limits of the allowed margins of fluctuation.

The simplest test of target zone credibility is not, however, appropriate to analyze the often claimed improvement in the credibility of EMS bands. The main purpose of this chapter has been to test those claims. For this purpose, we have explored data on forward excess returns.

Assuming that EMS exchange markets are efficient, one of the implications is that the forward excess returns should be white noise processes. However, simple plots of EMS data clearly contradict this implication. It appears that, besides the existence of some outliers, the *ex-post* forward excess returns contain a negative systematic component.

In an exchange rate system like the EMS, where exchange rates are managed within a band but where the band is shifted at times, persistent forward excess returns can be explained by the existence of a "peso problem" or a risk premium containing a systematic component.

If the EMS became a credible exchange rate system, there would be no room for "peso problems" nor for persistent risk premia. The transition from a non-credible to a credible EMS should, therefore, be accompanied by a move of the systematic forward excess return towards zero.

There is a set of events which were expected *a priori* to have positive implications for the credibility of the EMS, but whose effects do not show up in the investigation carried out in this study. The following can be mentioned:

(i) The convergence of EMS inflation rates towards the German inflation rate - a phenomenon which started three or four years after the launching of the EMS - was not translated into a decrease in the systematic forward excess return.

(ii) As noted in section 7.2, the realignments did not appear to be able to drive the expected exchange rates into the new fluctuation bands. This is confirmed in section 7.3 by the plots of the recursively estimated intercepts. In fact, after a realignment, no significant decrease in the systematic component of forward excess returns could be observed. An interpretation of this result is that even after a change in central parities, expectations of future changes were not abated.

(iii) The previous considerations also apply to the January 1987 realignment. Market participants did not consider it to be *the* last realignment.

(iv) The dismantling of foreign exchange controls started when the EMS was not credible. The dismantling did not, however, help improve credibility.

(v) The narrowing of the LIT/DM band in January 1990 was neither a decision based on the existence of a credible exchange rate, nor has it helped in improving the credibility of the central LIT/DM rate.

On the whole, the estimations carried out in this study did not show a significant shift in the systematic excess returns. The alleged improvement in the EMS target zone credibility is, thus, not validated.

CHAPTER 8
Summary and conclusions

In this book we present a critical assessment of the EMS in the 1980s and in the beginning of the 1990s.

In chapter 3 we analyze exchange market interventions by ERM central banks. In the design of the EMS, foreign exchange intervention is the only explicit instrument for keeping market exchange rates within the allowed margins of fluctuation. The analysis focuses on the first eight years of the EMS. During this period, the system was subject to eleven realignments which seems to question the ability of official foreign exchange intervention to affect market exchange rates.

The results show a clear conflict between external and internal objectives: In order to keep control over the money supply, ERM central banks sterilized foreign exchange intervention; this, in turn, made intervention unsuccessful and costly in terms of international reserves losses.

The inability of foreign exchange interventions to affect market exchange rates raises a question: How did Dutch monetary authorities keep the guilder within the same DM exchange rate band since March 1983? The answer to this question is found in chapters 4 and 5. On the one hand, we show in chapter 5 that the Netherlands lost the independence of its monetary policy. This is a condition for long-run stability of exchange rates. On the other hand, the Netherlands are the only member of the EMS that, through interest rate increases, has been able to recover international reserves and appreciate the domestic currency in a visible way; this is a condition for exchange-rate stability in the short run.

The poor results achieved by official foreign exchange intervention are not surprising in the case of the remaining ERM members; had intervention been an effective instrument for countering exchange rate trends, there would have been no need for the observed realignments. What might seem puzzling is that, despite those results, ERM member countries insisted in intervening and, simultaneously, sterilizing. The only explanation for this is given by the design of the EMS. While the rules of the system explicitly require the members to intervene, they do not specify that monetary convergence should be made towards Germany and, thus, do not prohibit the sterilization of foreign exchange interventions in the DM exchange market. This implies that the EMS countries have likely exchanged the stability in the stock of international reserves for monetary autonomy.

In chapter 5, it is shown that France and Italy followed independent monetary policies during most of the 1980s. This finding, together with the record of the inflation/unemployment trade-off, seems to question the "EMS discipline/ credibility hypotheses". The fact that at realignments high-inflation countries did not fully recover competitiveness losses led to assess, in chapter 6, whether active monetary policies in the EMS had perverse effects due to exchange rate constraints. The results show that in the inflation-prone members of the system, Italy and France, the temptation to create money surprises decreased after 1979. This conclusion applies specially to Italy. Self-imposed discipline is thus a characteristic of monetary policy in the EMS.

Combining the results of chapter 5 and chapter 6, we can conclude that, during most of the 1980s, the inflation-prone members of the EMS followed counterproductive policies: they repressed the adjustment of nominal exchange rates while following independent monetary policies.

The notion of a "New EMS" was analyzed in chapters 5 and 7. This label has been used to characterize the EMS after 1987: a system of credible exchange rates. The results from chapter 5 show that the period after 1987 is a period of convergence of policies among members of the EMS. This seems to validate the hypothesis of a "New EMS". However, both the results from chapter 7 and the turbulances in the system since September 1992 show that less independent monetary policies did not lead to clear improvements in exchange rate credibility. One explanation for this is that monetary authorities did not acquire a good enough reputation to make the public believe that policies would not be changed again to face the deep recession of Europe in the early 1990s.

Policymakers in Europe and elsewhere have praised the alleged success of the EMS as an instrument to gain credibility of low-inflation policies and achieve disinflation at low cost. This benign view of the EMS so much dominated the policy debate that policymakers, like many economists, had no other explanation for the breakdown of the EMS than the vicious activities of a small club of cynical speculators. This assessment rests on the assumption that credibility can be obtained through external constraints.

The empirical evidence presented in this study strongly points into the opposite direction: Credibility and its economic benefits can only be obtained through domestic policy changes. As the public sees through the weakness of the constraints a system like the EMS imposes on domestic policies, the hope that pegging the exchange rate alone makes good intentions credible remains an illusion.

References

Agénor, P. R., Bhandari, J., and Flood, R. (1991). "Speculative Attacks and Models of Balance-of-Payments Crises", NBER Working Paper No. 3919

Alesina, A. (1989). "Politics and Business Bycles in Industrial Democracies", *Economic Policy*, No. 8, pp. 55-98.

Almekinders, G. and Eijffinger, S. (1991). "Empirical Evidence on Foreign Exchange Market Intervention: Where Do We Stand?", *Weltwirtschaftliches Archiv*, Vol. 127, No. 4, pp. 645-677.

Artis, M. J. and Nachane, D. (1990). "Wages and Prices in Europe: A Test of the German Leadership Thesis", *Weltwirtschaftliches Archiv*, Vol. 126, No. 1, pp. 59-77.

Artis, M. J. and Taylor, M. P. (1988). "Exchange Rates, Interest Rates, Capital Controls and the European Monetary System: Assessing the Track Record", in F. Giavazzi, S. Micossi and M. Miller (eds.), *"The European Monetary System"*, Cambridge: Cambridge University Press.

Artus, J. R. (1976). "Exchange Rate Stability and Managed Floating: the Experience of the FRG", *IMF Staff Papers*, Vol. 23, pp. 312-333.

Barro, R. (1978). "Unanticipated Money, Output, and the Price Level in the United States", *Journal of Political Economy*, Vol. 86, pp. 549-580.

Barro, R. and Gordon, D. (1983a). "A Positive Theory of Monetary Policy in a Natural Rate Model", *Journal of Political Economy*, Vol. 91, No. 4, pp. 589-610.

Barro, R. and Gordon, D. (1983b). "Rules, Discretion, and Reputation in a Model of Monetary Policy", *Journal of Monetary Economics*, Vol. 12, pp. 101-121.

Begg, D. (1988). Comment on "The Advantage of Tying One's Hands: The EMS Discipline and Central Bank Credibility" by F. Giavazzi and M. Pagano, *European Economic Review*, Vol. 32, pp. 1075-1077.

Bernanke, B. S. (1986). "Alternative Explanations of the Money-Income Correlation", NBER Working Paper No. 1842.

Bertola, G. and Svensson, L. E. O. (1990). "Stochastic Devaluation Risk and the Empirical Fit of Target-Zone Models", Institute for International Economic Studies, Stockholm University, Seminar Paper No. 481.

Blanchard, O. (1989). "A Traditional Interpretation of Macroeconomic Fluctuations", *American Economic Review*, Vol. 79, No. 5, pp. 1146-1164.

Blanchard, O. and Muet, P. (1993). "Competitiveness Through Disinflation: An Assessment of the French Macroeconomic Strategy", *Economic Policy*, No. 16, pp. 11-56, Cambridge: Cambridge University Press.

Blanchard, O. and Watson, M. (1984). "Are Business Cycles All Alike?", NBER Working Paper No. 1392.

Blanco, H. and Garber, P. (1986). "Recurrent Devaluation and Speculative Attacks on the Mexican Peso", *Journal of Political Economy*, Vol. 94, No. 1, pp. 148-166.

Blejer, M. (1977). "The Short-Run Dynamics of Prices and the Balance of Payments", *American Economic Review*, Vol. 67, No. 3, pp. 419-428.

Bordo, M. and Schwartz, A. (1990). "What Has Foreign Exchange Market Intervention Since the Plaza Agreement Accomplished?", NBER Working Paper No. 3562.

Borensztein, E. (1987). "Alternative Hypothesis About the Excess Return of Dollar Assets", *IMF Staff Papers*, Vol. 34, pp. 29-59.

Branson, W. (1988). Comment on "The Role of the Exchange-rate Regime in a Disinflation: Empirical Evidence on the European Monetary System" by F. Giavazzi and A. Giovannini, in F. Giavazzi, S. Micossi and M. Miller (eds.), *"The European Monetary System"*, Cambridge: Cambridge University Press. pp. 108-111.

Branson, W. (1994). Comment on "European Exchange Rate Credibility Before the Fall" by A. Rose and L. E. O. Svensson, *European Economic Review*, Vol. 38, No. 6, pp. 1217-1220.

Branson, W. H., Halttunen, H., and Masson, P. (1977). "Exchange Rates in the Short Run", *European Economic Review*, Vol. 10, pp. 303-324.

Branson, W. H., Halttunen, H., and Masson, P. (1979). "Exchange Rates in the Short Run - Some Further Results", *European Economic Review*, Vol. 12, pp. 395-402.

Breusch, T. S. (1978). "Testing for Autocorrelation in Dynamic Linear Models", *Australian Economic Papers*, Vol. 17, pp. 334-355.

Burdekin, R. and Burkett, P. (1990). "A Re-examination of the Monetary Model of Exchange Market Pressure: Canada, 1963-1988", *The Review of Economics and Statistics*, Vol. 72, No. 4, pp. 677-681.

Calvo, G. (1978). "On the Time Consistency of Optimal Policy in a Monetary Economy", *Econometrica*, Vol. 46, pp. 1411-1428.

Canzoneri, M. and Henderson, D. (1988). "Is Sovereign Policymaking Bad?" in K. Brunner and A. Meltzer (eds.), "Stabilization Policies and Labor Markets", *Carnegie-Rochester Conference Series on Public Policy*, Vol. 28, pp. 193-235, Amsterdam: North-Holland.

Collins, S. M. (1988). "Inflation and the European Monetary System", in F. Giavazzi, S. Micossi and M. Miller (eds.), *"The European Monetary System"*, Cambridge: Cambridge University Press.

Commission of the European Communities (1979). "The European Monetary System - Commentary and Documents", *European Economy*, No. 3 (July), pp. 63-111.

Commission of the European Communities (1983). *European Economy*, No. 18.

Commission of the European Communities (1990). "Monetary Coordination in Stage I of EMU", *European Economy*, No. 46, pp. 182-186.

Commission of the European Communities (1991). "Money market developments and the functioning of the ERM during the first year of Stage I", *European Economy*, No. 50, pp. 195-210.

Cooley, T. F. and LeRoy, S. F. (1985). "Atheoretical Macroeconomics - A Critique", *Journal of Monetary Economics*, Vol. 16, pp. 283-308.

Cumby, R. and Van Wijnbergen, S. (1989). "Financial Policy and Speculative Runs with a Crawling Peg: Argentina 1979-1981", *Journal of International Economics*, Vol. 27, pp. 111-127.

Cushman, D. (1986). "Has Exchange Risk Depressed International Trade? The Impact of Third Country Exchange Risk", *Journal of International Money and Finance*, Vol. 5, pp. 361-380.

De Cecco, M. (1989). "The European Monetary System and National Interests" in P. Guerrieri and P. Padoan (eds.), *"The Political Economy of European Integration"*, London: Harvester-Wheatsheaf.

De Grauwe, P. (1987). "International Trade and Economic Growth in the European Monetary System", *European Economic Review*, Vol. 31, pp. 389-398.

De Grauwe, P. (1989). *"International Money: Post-War Trends and Theories"*, Oxford: Oxford University Press.

De Grauwe, P. (1990). "The Cost of Disinflation and the European Monetary System", *Open Economies Review*, Vol. 1, pp. 147-173.

Dickey, D. A. and Fuller, W. A. (1981). "Likelihood Ratio Statistics for Autoregressive Time Series With a Unit Root", *Econometrica*, Vol. 49, No. 4, pp. 1057-1072.

Dominguez, K. (1986). "Does Sterilized Intervention Influence Exchange Rates? A Test of the Signalling Hypothesis", *mimeo*, Department of Economics, Yale University.

Dominguez, K. and Frankel, J. (1990). "Does Foreign Exchange Intervention Matter? Disentangling the Portfolio and Expectations Effect for the Mark", NBER Working Paper No. 3299, Cambridge, MA.

Dominguez, K. and Frankel, J. (1993). "Does Foreign-Exchange Intervention Matter? The Portfolio Effect", *American Economic Review*, Vol. 83, No. 5, pp. 1356-1369.

Driffill, J. (1988). "The Stability and Sustainability of the European Monetary System With Perfect Capital Markets", in F. Giavazzi, S. Micossi and M. Miller (eds.), *"The European Monetary System"*, Cambridge: Cambridge University Press.

Engle, R. F. and Granger, C. W. J. (1987). "Co-integration and Error Correction: Representation, Estimation, and Testing", *Econometrica*, Vol. 55, No. 2, pp. 251-276.

Evans, M. and Lewis, K. (1993). "Trends in Excess Returns in Currency and Bond Markets", *European Economic Review*, Vol. 37, No. 5, pp. 1005-1019.

Flood, R., Rose, A., and Mathieson, D. (1990). "Is the EMS the Perfect Fix? An Empirical Exploration of Exchange Rate Target Zones", Board of Governors of the Federal Reserve System, International Finance Discussion Papers, No. 388 (unpublished).

Frankel, J. (1979). "On the Mark: A Theory of Floating Exchange Rates Based on Real Interest Differentials", *American Economic Review*, Vol. 69, No. 4, pp. 610-622.

Frankel, J. and Phillips, S. (1991), "The European Monetary System: Credible At Last?", NBER Working Paper No. 3819.

Frankel, J., Phillips, S. and Chinn, M. (1993). "Financial and Currency Integration in the European Monetary System: The Statistical Record", in F. Torres and F. Giavazzi (eds.), *"Adjustment and Growth in the European Monetary Union"*, Cambridge: Cambridge University Press.

Fratianni, M. (1988). "The European Monetary System: How Well Has It Worked?", *The Cato Journal*, Vol. 8, pp. 477-501.

Fratianni, M. and von Hagen, J. (1990a). "The European Monetary System Ten Years After", in K. Brunner and A. Meltzer (eds.), "Unit Roots, Investment Measures and Other Essays", *Carnegie-Rochester Conference Series on Public Policy*, Vol. 32, pp. 173-250, Amsterdam: North-Holland.

Fratianni, M. and von Hagen, J. (1990b). "Asymmetries and Realignments in the EMS", in P. De Grauwe and L. Papademos (eds.) *"The European Monetary System in the 1990s"*, London: Longman.

Fratianni, M. and von Hagen, J. (1990c). "German Dominance in the EMS: The Empirical Evidence", *Open Economies Review*, Vol. 1, pp. 67-87.

Fratianni, M. and von Hagen, J. (1990d). "Credibility and Asymmetries in the EMS", in V. Argy and P. De Grauwe (eds.), *"Choosing an Exchange Rate Regime - The Challenge for Smaller Industrial Countries"*, Washington: International Monetary Fund.

Gardner, E. and Perraudin, W. (1993). "Asymmetry in the ERM - A Case Study of French and German Interest Rates Before and After German Unification", *IMF Staff Papers*, Vol. 40, No. 2, pp. 427-450.

Gärtner, M. (1987). "Intervention Policy under Floating Exchange Rates: An Analysis of the Swiss Case", *Economica*, Vol. 54, pp. 439-453.

Genberg, H. (1981). "Effects of Central Bank Intervention in the Foreign Exchange Market", *IMF Staff Papers*, Vol. 28, No. 3, pp. 451-476.

Giavazzi, F. (1989). "The Exchange Rate Question in Europe", in R. Bryant, D. Currie, J. Frenkel, P. Masson and R. Portes (eds.), *"Macroeconomic Policies in an Interdependent World"*, Washington: International Monetary Fund.

Giavazzi, F. and Giovannini, A. (1986). "The EMS and the Dollar", *Economic Policy*, No. 2, pp. 456-485, Cambridge: Cambridge University Press.

Giavazzi, F. and Giovannini, A. (1988). "The Role of the Exchange-Rate Regime in a Disinflation: Empirical Evidence on the European Monetary System", in F. Giavazzi, S. Micossi and M. Miller (eds.), *"The European Monetary System"*, Cambridge: Cambridge University Press.

Giavazzi, F. and Giovannini, A. (1989). *"Limiting Exchage Rate Flexibility - The European Monetary System"*, Cambridge, Mass.: MIT Press.

Giavazzi, F. and Pagano, M. (1988). "The Advantage of Tying One's Hands - EMS Discipline and Central Bank Credibility", *European Economic Review*, Vol. 32, pp. 1055-1082.

Giavazzi, F. and Spaventa, L. (1990). "The'new' EMS", in P. De Grauwe and L. Papademos (eds.) *"The European Monetary System in the 1990s"*, London: Longman.

Giovannini, A. (1989). "How do Fixed-Exchange-Rate Regimes Work? Evidence From the Gold Standard, Bretton Woods and the EMS", in M. Miller, B. Eichengreen and R. Portes, *"Blueprints for Exchange-Rate Management"*, London: Academic Press.

Girton, L. and Roper, D. (1977). "A Monetary Model of Exchange Market Pressure Applied to the Postwar Canadian Experience", *American Economic Review*, Vol. 67, pp. 537-548.

Glick, R. and Wihlborg, C. (1990). "Real Exchange Rate Effects of Monetary Shocks under Fixed and Flexible Exchange Rates", *Journal of International Economics*, Vol. 28, No. 3/4, pp. 267-290.

Godfrey, L. G. (1978). "Testing for Higher Order Serial Correlation in Regression Equations When the Regressors Include Lagged Dependent Variables", *Econometrica*, Vol. 46, pp. 1303-1310.

Goldberg, L. (1990). "Predicting Exchange Rate Crises: Mexico Revisited", NBER Working Paper No. 3320.

Gordon, R. and King, S. (1982). "The Output Cost of Disinflation in Traditional and Vector Autoregressive Models", *Brookings Papers on Economic Activity*, No. 82:1.

Grilli, V. (1989). "Seigniorage in Europe", in M. De Cecco and A. Giovannini (eds.), *"A European Central Bank? Perspectives on Monetary Unification After Ten Years of the EMS"*, Cambridge: Cambridge University Press.

Gros, D. (1989). "On the Volatility of Exchange Rates: Tests of Monetary and Portfolio Balance Models of Exchange Rate Determination", *Weltwirtschaftliches Archiv*, Vol. 125, No. 2, pp. 273-295.

Gros, D. (1990). "Seigniorage and EMS discipline", in P. De Grauwe and L. Papademos (eds.), *"The European Monetary System in the 1990's"*, pp. 162-178, Longman.

Gros, D. (1992). "Capital Controls and Foreign Exchange Market Crises in the EMS", *European Economic Review*, Vol. 36, No. 8, pp. 1533-1544.

Gros, D. and Thygesen, N. (1992). *"European Monetary Integration - From the European Monetary System to European Monetary Union"*, London: Longman.

Hall, S. G. (1986). "An Application of the Granger and Engle Two-step Estimation Procedure to United Kingdom Aggregate Wage Data", *Oxford Bulletin of Economics and Statistics*, Vol. 48, No. 3, pp. 229-239.

Hamilton, J. (1983). "Oil and the Macroeconomy since World War II", *Journal of Political Economy*, Vol. 91, No. 2, pp. 228-248.

Hansen, L. P. and Hodrick, R. (1980). "Forward Exchange Rates as Optimal Predictors of Future Spot Rates: An Econometric Analysis", *Journal of Political Economy*, Vol. 88, No. 5, pp. 829-853.

Hendry, D. (1989). *"PC-Give: An Interactive Econometric Modelling System"*, University of Oxford.

Herring, R. and Marston, R. (1977). "Sterilisation Policy: the Trade-off between Monetary Autonomy and Control Over Foreign Exchange Reserves", *European Economic Review*, Vol. 10, pp. 325-343.

Hodgson, J. and Schneck, R. (1981). "Stability of the Relationship between Monetary Variables and Exchange Market Pressure: Empirical Evidence", *Southern Economic Journal*, Vol. 47, No. 4, pp. 941-958.

Hughes-Hallett, A., Minford, P., and Rastogi, A. (1990). "The European Monetary System - Achievements and Survival", Liverpool Research Group in Macro-economics, University of Liverpool, Working Paper No. 90/04.

IMF (1984). "Exchange Rate Volatility and World Trade", Research Department of the IMF, Occasional Paper No. 28, Washington: International Monetary Fund.

Joyce, J. (1986). "Canadian Exchange Market Intervention and Domestic Monetary Operations", *Quarterly Review of Economics and Business*, Vol. 26, No. 2, pp. 94-105.

Jung, A. C. and Wieland, V. (1990). "Forward Rates and Spot Rates in the European Monetary System - Forward Market Efficiency", *Weltwirtschaftliches Archiv*, Vol. 126, No. 4, pp. 615-629.

Kamas, L. (1986). "The Balance of Payments Offset to Monetary Policy: Monetarist, Portfolio Balance, and Keynesian Estimates for Mexico and Venezuela", *Journal of Money, Credit, and Banking*, Vol. 18, No. 4, pp. 467-481.

Kaminsky, G. and Peruga, R. (1991). "Credibility Crises: The Dollar in the Early 1980s", *Journal of International Money and Finance*, Vol. 10, pp. 170-192.

Kearney, C. and MacDonald, R. (1986). "Intervention and Sterilisation under Floating Exchange Rates", *European Economic Review*, Vol. 30, pp. 345-364.

Kenen, P. B. (1987). "Exchange Rate Management: What Role for Intervention?", *American Economic Review*, Vol. 77, No. 2, pp. 194-199.

Koedijk, K. and Kool, C. (1992). "Dominant interest and inflation differentials within the EMS", *European Economic Review*, Vol. 36, No. 4, pp. 925-943.

Kostiainen, S. and Taimio, H. (1988). "Interest Rate Policy With Expectations of Devaluation", *Scandinavian Journal of Economics*, Vol. 90, No. 2, pp. 211-224.

Kouri, P. and Porter, M. (1974). "International Capital Flows and Portfolio Equilibrium", *Journal of Political Economy*, Vol. 82, No. 3, pp. 443-467.

Krasker, W. (1980). "The 'Peso Problem' in Testing the Efficiency of Forward Exchange Markets", *Journal of Monetary Economics*, Vol. 6, pp. 269-276.

Kremers, J. (1990). "Gaining Policy Credibility for a Disinflation - Ireland's Experience in the EMS", *IMF Staff Papers*, Vol. 37, No.1 (March), pp. 116-145.

Krugman, P. (1991). "Target Zones and Exchange Rate Dynamics", *The Quarterly Journal of Economics*, Vol. 106, No. 3, pp. 669-682.

Kydland, F. and Prescott, E. (1977). "Rules Rather than Discretion: The Inconsistency of Optimal Plans", *Journal of Political Economy*, Vol. 85, No. 3, pp. 473-491.

Lewis, K. (1989). "Changing Beliefs and Systematic Rational Forecast Errors with Evidence from Foreign Exchange", *American Economic Review*, Vol. 79, No. 4, pp. 621-636.

Litterman, R. and Weiss, L. (1985). "Money, Real Interest Rates, and Output: A Reinterpretation of Postwar U.S. Data", *Econometrica*, Vol. 53, No. 1, pp. 129-156.

Lizondo, J. (1983). "Foreign Exchange Futures Prices Under Fixed Exchange Rates", *Journal of International Economics*, Vol. 14, pp. 69-84.

Longworth, D. (1980). "Canadian Intervention in the Foreign Exchange Market: a Note", *The Review of Economics and Statistics*, Vol. 62, pp. 284-287.

Lucas, R. (1976). "Econometric Policy Evaluation: A Critique", *Carnegie-Rochester Conference Series on Public Policy*, Vol. 1, pp. 19-46.

Lütkepohl, H. (1990). "Asymptotic Distributions of Impulse Response Functions and Forecast Error Variance Decompositions of Vector Autoregressive Models", *Review of Economic Studies*, Vol. LXXII, No. 1, pp. 116-125.

MacDonald, R. and Taylor, M. (1991). "Exchange Rates, Policy Convergence, and the European Monetary System", *The Review of Economics and Statistics*, Vol. 73, No. 3, pp. 553-558.

Mastropasqua, C., Micossi, S., and Rinaldi, R. (1988). "Interventions, Sterilisation and Monetary Policy in European Monetary System Countries, 1979-87", in F. Giavazzi, S. Micossi and M. Miller (eds.), *"The European Monetary System"*, Cambridge: Cambridge University Press.

Mélitz, J. (1988). "Monetary Discipline and Cooperation in the EMS: A Synthesis", in F. Giavazzi, S. Micossi and M. Miller (eds.), *"The European Monetary System"*, Cambridge: Cambridge University Press.

Minford, P. (1989). "Exchange-Rate Regimes and Policy Coordination", in M. Miller, B. Eichengreen and R. Portes, *"Blueprints for Exchange-Rate Management"*, London: Academic Press.

Mussa, M. (1981). "The Role of Official Intervention", Group of Thirty Occasional Papers, No. 6, New York: Group of Thirty.

Neumann, M. and von Hagen, J. (1993). "Monetary Policy in the G-7 Countries - Germany", in M. Fratianni and D. Salvatore (eds.), *"Monetary Policy in Developed Economies"*, Westport: Greenwood Press.

Obstfeld, M. (1982). "Can We Sterilise? Theory and Evidence", *American Economic Review*, Vol. 72, No. 2, pp. 45-50.

Obstfeld, M. (1983). "Exchange Rates, Inflation, and the Sterilisation Problem", *European Economic Review*, Vol. 21, pp. 161-202.

Obstfeld, M. (1988). "Competitiveness, Realignment, and Speculation: The Role of Financial Markets", in F. Giavazzi, S. Micossi and M. Miller (eds.), *"The European Monetary System"*, Cambridge: Cambridge University Press.

Obstfeld, M. (1991). "Destabilizing Effects of Exchange-Rate Escape Clauses", NBER Working Paper No. 3603.

Østrup, F. (1992). *"The Development of the European Monetary System"*, Copenhaguen: Jurist og Økonomforbundets Forlag.

Papademos, L. (1990). "Greece and the EMS: Issues, Prospects and a Framework for Analysis", in P. De Grauwe and L. Papademos (eds.) *"The European Monetary System in the 1990s"*, London: Longman.

Penati, A. and Pennacchi, G. (1989). "Optimal Portfolio Choice and the Collapse of a Fixed-Exchange Rate Regime", *Journal of International Economics*, Vol. 27, pp. 1-24.

Persson, T. (1987). "Credibility of Macroeconomic Policy: An Introduction and a Broad Survey", Institute for International Economic Studies, Sweden, Working Paper No. 107. Also in *European Economic Review*, March 1988.

Quirk, P. J. (1977). "Exchange Rate Policy in Japan: Leaning Against the Wind", *IMF Staff Papers*, Vol. 24, No. 3, pp. 642-664.

Rogoff, K. (1985a). "The Optimal Degree of Commitment to an Intermediate Monetary Target", *The Quarterly Journal of Economics*, Vol. 100, No. 4, pp. 1169-1189.

Rogoff, K. (1985b). "Can Exchange Rate Predictability Be Achieved Without Monetary Convergence? Evidence from the EMS", *European Economic Review*, Vol. 28, pp. 93-115.

Roper, D. E. and Turnovsky, S. J. (1980). "Optimal Exchange Market Intervention in a Simple Stochastic Macro Model", *Canadian Journal of Economics*, Vol. 13, No. 2, pp. 296-309.

Rose, A. and Svensson, L. E. O. (1991). "Expected and Predicted Realignments: The FF/DM Exchange Rate During the EMS", NBER Working Paper No. 3685.

Rose, A. and Svensson, L. E. O. (1994). "European Exchange Rate Credibility Before the Fall", *European Economic Review*, Vol. 38, No. 6, pp. 1185-1216.

Russo, M. and Tullio, G. (1988). "Monetary Policy Coordination within the European Monetary System: Is There a Rule?", in F. Giavazzi, S. Micossi and M. Miller (eds.), *"The European Monetary System"*, Cambridge: Cambridge University Press.

Salop, J. (1981). "The Divergence Indicator: A Technical Note", *IMF Staff Papers*, Vol. 28, No. 4, pp. 682-697.

Sims, C. A. (1980a). "Macroeconomics and Reality", *Econometrica*, Vol. 48, No.1, pp. 1-48.

Sims, C. A. (1980b). "Comparison of Interwar and Postwar Business Cycles: Monetarism Reconsidered", *American Economic Review*, Vol. 70, No. 2, pp. 250-257.

Sjöö, B. (1987). "IMF Data on Tape: Introduction and Manual to the READIFS Programs", *mimeo*, Department of Economics, School of Economics and Commercial Law, Gothenburg University.

Spencer, D. E. (1989). "Does Money Matter? The Robustness of Evidence From Vector Autoregressions", *Journal of Money, Credit, and Banking*, Vol. 21, No. 4, pp. 442-454.

Svensson, L. E. O. (1991a). "The Simplest Test of Target Zone Credibility", *IMF Staff Papers*, Vol. 38, pp. 655-665.

Svensson, L. E. O. (1991b). "Assessing Target Zone Credibility: Mean Reversion and Devaluation Expectations in the EMS", Centre for Economic Policy Research, Discussion Paper No. 580.

Tabellini, G. (1994). Comment on "European Exchange Rate Credibility Before the Fall" by A. Rose and L. E. O. Svensson, *European Economic Review*, Vol. 38, No. 6, pp. 1221-1223.

Torres, F. (1990). "Portugal, the EMS and 1992: Stabilization and Liberalization", in P. De Grauwe and L. Papademos (eds.) *"The European Monetary System in the 1990s"*, London: Longman.

Ungerer, H.; Evans, O. and Nyberg, P. (1983). "The European Monetary System: The Experience, 1979-82", IMF Occasional Paper No. 19 (May), Washington, D. C.: International Monetary Fund.

Ungerer, H.; Evans, O.; Mayer, T. and Young, P. (1986). "The European Monetary System: Recent Developments", IMF Occasional Paper No. 48 (December), Washington, D. C.: International Monetary Fund.

Ungerer, H.; Hauvonen, J.; Lopez-Claros, A. and Mayer, T. (1990). "The European Monetary System: Developments and Perspectives", IMF Occasional Paper No. 73 (November), Washington, D. C.: International Monetary Fund.

Van Ypersele, J. (1985). *"The European Monetary System: Origins, Operation and Outlook"*, Brussels: Commission of the European Communities.

Viñals, J. (1990). "The EMS, Spain and Macroeconomic Policy", in P. De Grauwe and L. Papademos (eds.) *"The European Monetary System in the 1990s"*, London: Longman.

von Hagen, J. (1989). "Monetary Targeting with Exchange Rate Constraints: The Bundesbank in the 1980s", *The Federal Reserve Bank of St Louis Review*, Vol. 71, No. 5 (September/October), pp. 53-69.

von Hagen, J. (1993). "Monetary Policy Coordination in the European Monetary System", in M. Fratianni and D. Salvatore (eds.), *"Monetary Policy in Developed Economies"*, pp. 509-560, Westport: Greenwood Press.

von Hagen, J. and Fratianni, M. (1990). "German Dominance in the EMS: Evidence from Interest Rates", *Journal of International Money and Finance*, Vol 9, No. 4, pp. 358-375.

Vona, S. and Bini-Smaghi, L. (1988). "Economic Growth and Exchange Rates in the European Monetary System: Their Trade Effects in a Changing External Environment", in F. Giavazzi, S. Micossi and M. Miller (eds.), *"The European Monetary System"*, Cambridge: Cambridge University Press.

Wihlborg, C. and Willett, T. (1990). "The Instability of Half-Way Measures in the Transition To a Common Currency", Gothenburg Studies in Financial Economics, No. 90:13, Gothenburg University.

Wyplosz, C. (1989). "Asymmetry in the EMS: Intentional or Systemic?", *European Economic Review*, Vol. 33, pp. 310-320.

Subject index

Figures

Tables

Printing: Weihert-Druck GmbH, Darmstadt
Binding: Theo Gansert Buchbinderei GmbH, Weinheim